"I have worked with Sandra for several years, and can speak genuinely for her well intentioned heart and desire to help others. "The Power Of Conscious Living" is a truly helpful book for people from all walks of life who want to start taking control of their lives. Sandra explains the concepts and science behind a holistic lifestyle, backed up by research from the very best spiritual teachers and healers, in an easy to understand and comprehensive way. I am sure it will be an invaluable tool for all those who are drawn to read this special book"

Claire Montanaro,
author of "Spiritual Wisdom"

How to **RECREATE YOUR LIFE** and
FIND THE KEY TO TRUE HAPPINESS

The Power of
CONSCIOUS
LIVING Sandra
Kendrew

BALBOA.
PRESS

A DIVISION OF HAY HOUSE

Balboa Press books may be ordered through booksellers or by contacting:

Balboa Press
A Division of Hay House
1663 Liberty Drive
Bloomington, IN 47403
www.balboapress.com
1-(877) 407-4847

Because of the dynamic nature of the Internet, any web addresses or links contained in this book may have changed since publication and may no longer be valid. The views expressed in this work are solely those of the author and do not necessarily reflect the views of the publisher, and the publisher hereby disclaims any responsibility for them.

The author of this book does not dispense medical advice or prescribe the use of any technique as a form of treatment for physical, emotional, or medical problems without the advice of a physician, either directly or indirectly. The intent of the author is only to offer information of a general nature to help you in your quest for emotional and spiritual well-being. In the event you use any of the information in this book for yourself, which is your constitutional right, the author and the publisher assume no responsibility for your actions.

Any people depicted in stock imagery provided by Thinkstock are models, and such images are being used for illustrative purposes only.
Certain stock imagery © Thinkstock.

ISBN: 978-1-4525-4447-2 (sc)
ISBN: 978-1-4525-4414-4 (hc)
ISBN: 978-1-4525-4413-7 (e)

Library of Congress Control Number: 2011963741

Printed in the United States of America

Balboa Press rev. date: 02/27/2012

This book is written for you!

"The greatest gift that you can give to others is the gift of unconditional love and acceptance"

Brian Tracy

"You must be the change you want to see in the world"

Mahatma Gandhi

Acknowledgements

A big thank you to my husband David, for his love, patience, support, belief in me and for allowing me the space to do my work over the last thirty five years! At least you have learnt to cook competently without my input and long may it last!

I am blessed and very proud of my children Nick, Charlotte and Hollie, plus grandchildren, who have shown me the true meaning of unconditional love. Thank you for all your support, for having the confidence in me to write this book and for just being there.

Thank you to my mum, Jean, and dad, Bill, (who I know is watching over me). I know I chose well. Your guidance, love, continued support and encouragement allowed me to follow my heart. Also Marjorie and Charles, for their wisdom, amazing knowledge and memories.

Thank you to my sisters Loraine and Julie, who fortunately are on my wavelength! and for their great faith in me to write this book. I have enjoyed the hours we have spent together discussing the world and life!

After many years spent talking about this book, we have "made it," so many thanks to Ruth Badley, a friend, PR and Editor. I have really valued your skills with the written word, the input, time, patience and instant grasp of the content of this book, and your ability to respond to my emails is unbelievable!

Thank you to my close "yoga group," Anne, Yvonne and Margaret who have been pushing me for over ten years to write a book. Thanks for all your support, and the confidence you have shown in my ability is really appreciated.

To all my teachers, especially, Claire Montanaro, Mike Robinson and Caitlin Walsh. You have contributed to my "awakening," understanding of life and have pushed me to trust in myself – a massive thank you.

To all my other close friends and clients who have shared my journey, and allowed me to be part of their lives.

To John Moss and Helen Lamb at the British Society of Dowsers, thank you for all your co-operation and support in the past, and allowing me to use your illustrations on dowsing.

The biggest push to move out of my comfort zone, write this book and spread my knowledge came from Sonia Choquette, a brilliant American author and spiritual teacher, so an immense thank you for giving me the confidence that I Can Do It!

This book was assembled from my own experiences and work, from published scientific literature, spiritual teachers and authors who have allowed me to quote from their own research and books. I am eternally grateful for all your kindness and support. With infinite love and gratitude to the following:

Dr Deepak Chopra, Dr Harry Oldfield, Dr Bruce Lipton, Professor Chris Sinha, Eckhart Tolle, Mike Robinson, Rolf Gordon, Elizabeth Brown, Lynne McTaggart, Claire Montanaro, Dr Masaro Emoto, Dr John Briffa, Dr Joseph Mercola, Miriam Young, Dr Norman Shealy, John Ruskan, Dr Susan Cabot, Dr Ron Rosedale, Dr Malcolm Kendrick, Erin H. Shackell, Lionel G. Standing, Patrick Holford, Peter Russell and Dr Wayne Dyer

Table of Contents

List of Illustrations

Preface

Natural forces within us are the healers of disease
Hippocrates

Every situation perceived properly becomes an opportunity to heal
Helen Schucman founder of "A Course in Miracles"

The true sign of intelligence is not knowledge but imagination
Albert Einstein

My Journey

This book is about self-empowerment and being the creator of your own reality, the only way of living. It offers truth about the self, allowing you to live in joy, freedom, and in the present moment. In this way, understanding how you *can* take control of your life **by being conscious** becomes clear.

Do you wake every morning and embrace the day with joy and peace in your heart? Or do you wake up feeling tired, depressed, dreading the day ahead, and feeling that your life is missing something? If the latter sounds more like you most of the time, then read on. Life is for living, not just existing!

My healing journey began after I was diagnosed with Irritable Bowel Syndrome (IBS) about thirty years ago and advised to take an anti-depressant. In my late twenties, with two children under eighteen months and suffering excruciating pain, it was tempting to take the advice, but a small inner voice kept urging me to "look inside." I knew I had to treat the cause of what triggered my IBS, and so many illnesses nowadays-EMOTIONAL STRESS!

So why was I stressed? I had a loving, supportive family.

Worry, like all negative emotions, is based on conditioning and beliefs and generally involves fear of the past or fear of the future. The past is gone and no one knows what the future holds. There is only this moment, the Now! And this was my breakthrough, my Eureka moment.

Now is all we have so get on and enjoy it! None of us know what can happen in the next minute, let alone the next day. Live each day as if it is your last! Life is not meant to be a struggle.

I felt compelled to step out of my comfort zone and write this book and I have Sonia Choquette, New York Times best selling author to thank for giving me the confidence to do this. With my knowledge she suggested I wrote about constellation healing. This is nothing to do with the stars but rather a collection of all I have learnt - a book which brings my work as an eclectic practitioner together.

Sonia Choquette is a world renowned author, healer and spiritual teacher. Her books have sold over a million copies worldwide, including her best seller, "The Answer is Simple." She helps people understand their soul's purpose and life plan.

I want to help others on a similar journey and show how you can change your thoughts, beliefs, and Rewrite Your Lifescript! I have included some useful exercises if you wish to participate in this journey of change, and I can guarantee, with practice, your life will operate from a place of joy and peace, instead of fear. We are all creators of our lives and no one else is responsible or to blame. You do not have to be a victim of anybody or anything.

Eventually through diet, yoga and various complementary therapies, my IBS disappeared. I had developed a milk allergy due to the impact of stress on my digestive system. The stress had to be tackled, but in the meantime I cut down my intake of dairy products by switching to alternatives such as rice milk. For extra calcium I chose broccoli, kale, salmon, sardines, nuts, seeds and dried beans, rather than dairy products. I also had acupuncture, reflexology and healing which I found helpful in rebalancing my energies.

A few years later my third child was born, and I retrained in various complementary therapies, including Reflexology, Psychotherapy, Life Coaching, Dowsing, Reiki and other forms of healing. My original studies over thirty years ago in Home Economics led me to specialise in Nutrition. I took part in a weekly radio programme for BBC Radio, and wrote regular features on diet and nutrition for local and national newspapers and magazines.

As an eclectic, intuitive practitioner I recognised that people in my home town could benefit from a dedicated Holistic Health Centre. My vision was to establish a safe environment where a range of fully qualified complementary therapists could run their own clinics from a central base. At the time this kind of complementary health centre was rarely found outside the bigger cities. As many therapies were relatively new I had to ensure client confidentiality and provide a safe environment.

There were around twenty practitioners working from the centre. These included some forward thinking general practitioners that offered homeopathy and acupuncture as part of their services. Many of the GPs in local practices would also refer patients to the Holistic Health Centre.

Every practitioner at the Centre had to have professional qualifications and valid insurance from their appropriate professional body. I also ran International Therapy Examination Council (ITEC) courses at weekends, so life became very busy. After about five years I sold the Centre and decided to concentrate on building up my own private practice.

Some twenty years ago I first learnt how to dowse and then latterly became interested in the phenomenon of Geopathic Stress. I was continually exhausted, until I called on the services of Dr Arthur Bailey PhD, and my health improved almost immediately. He was an engineering scientist who had an immense interest in dowsing and healing, which eventually overtook his academic career. Dr Bailey visited my home and rebalanced the geopathic stress within it. This occurs when the earth's natural radiation becomes distorted by weak, electromagnetic fields caused by underground water, mineral deposits, fault lines, construction, earthquakes and weather. In my work as "The House Healer" worldwide, I heal and rebalance energies within properties and work with the occupants to find the cause of their particular problems, through dowsing.

More importantly, I show them how to change their belief system and raise their consciousness, to ultimately allow them to create their own reality. This book is not exclusively about dowsing but there is a chapter explaining the process, as it certainly helps to develop intuition and demonstrates the power of the subconscious mind. For more information on the work I do see www.thehousehealer.co.uk

In this book I will be sharing ways of healing ourselves, others, our property and environment, and explain how to break free from the emotional turmoil which may hinder a full and swift recovery from illness.

We can influence our life by having positive thoughts which can raise our energy or consciousness, but it is not just about saying positive affirmations. First we must remove the debris of our conditioning and beliefs, *then,* positive thinking will have an impact.

Developing an awareness of the busy mind is needed to encourage change and to stop the endless circle of negative thoughts. Trust your intuition and act on it, without becoming attached to the outcome, otherwise the ego takes over.

CHANGE YOUR THOUGHTS AND BELIEFS

AND YOU CHANGE THE WORLD!

WHAT IS WITHIN IS WITHOUT

We need to learn how to dance with life, be childlike and have fun. When we are born, we are pure essence, no negative thoughts, no ego, no fears, only loving souls. Then conditioning by society takes over. We need to go back to basics, go with the flow and clear the patterns of the subconscious mind to find inner peace and the abundant fulfilling lives we are meant to have!

To enhance your healing and journey in life, I suggest keeping a daily journal to record feelings, emotions, thoughts, actions, both negative and positive, and anything else you consider important.

REGAIN YOUR LIFE

Chapter 1

Energy and The Field

Zero Point Field

The existence of the Zero Point Energy Field has been known in quantum science since Albert Einstein discovered it in 1913, but most scientists ignored its relevance. This subatomic field is a mass of quantum energy, which holds energy from which everything comes.

Lynne McTaggart, an award winning American journalist living in England, says in her book, "The Field":

"For a number of decades respected scientists all over the world have been carrying out well designed experiments whose results fly in the face of current biology and physics. What they have discovered is nothing less than astonishing. At our most elemental, we are not a chemical reaction, but an energetic charge. Human beings and all living things are a coalescence of energy in a field of energy connected to every other living thing in the world. This pulsating energy field is the central engine of our being and our consciousness, the alpha and omega of our existence"

It has been discovered that top scientists such as Peter Russell, a fellow of The Institute of Noetic Sciences, which I recommend referring to, says:

"We are all in this together-we are all connected. We are all part of a global consciousness-a universal consciousness"

Human beings have quantum energy within them that is constantly exchanging messages with this bigger sea of energy throughout the universe. The Chinese recognised this energy field as *chi* or *qi*. Other names used for it are *life force energy, prana or universal energy.*

This concept of our universe has fields of energy creating forces and interacting with each other. We have all experienced the situation where the phone has rung and we know who it is, or we sense the phone is going to ring, and then it does. The same overpowering feeling can overtake a parent who knows instinctively when their child may have a problem.

All this can be explained scientifically by the Field theory. We can sense the energy within a room, where our energy interacts. We can pick up the atmosphere in a room if there has been an argument. The saying *"you could cut the air with a knife"* or *"there's a chill in the air"* is a way of sensing something isn't right and the messages in the energy are being relayed and picked up.

When the Large Hadron Collider was installed I was a little apprehensive as to what might transpire.

I was nearing completion of this book when I noticed an article in the Sunday Times published on the 25th September 2011, with the headline, "Has Einstein's Speed Limit Been Broken?" The gist of the article suggested scientists had found a particle that travels faster than light! I found it interesting that I had already made reference to the subatomic particles in Chapter 3, before this discovery was made public.

Consciousness

We and everything around us are consciousness, as are the earth and universe.

Consciousness is an awareness of our own thoughts, memories, feelings, senses and surroundings. It is being connected to the whole of reality, which then brings a deeper meaning and truth to our lives.

My aim is to raise consciousness by living in the present moment as a heart centred individual. Once we achieve a higher state of consciousness within us, we affect everyone around us and help raise their energy levels. By working on ourselves we are helping to heal the world, just by *being*.

Our own consciousness is like a radio, and the Zero Point Energy Field is the radio station, so once we learn how to fine tune this, we can pick up many signals and messages. We are much more powerful than we could ever imagine, with the ability to heal ourselves, others, and the environment. You are the creator of your life!

The Human body is made up of parts and organs, and each of the organs are made up of tissues. If we then magnified a sample of the tissue we would see millions of cells. Turning up the magnification we see cells contain molecules that are made up of atoms, which are made up of even smaller subatomic particles. These subatomic particles are made up of energy. We are pure energy! From the core of our being we emit energy in all directions in wave like patterns, a matrix of interwining energy connecting with everyone and everything.

Dr Gary Schwartz, Professor of Psychology and Neurology at the University of Arizona, carried out studies to provide evidence that consciousness is not restricted to the brain, but lives on, even when the brain is technically dead. Lynne McTaggart wrote:

"In an important study of cardiac arrest patients who had been clinically dead for several minutes (flat EEGs and no electric activity in the brain cortex), the patients reported clear cognitive functioning, emotions, a sense of identity, and memories from early childhood as well as perception from a location out of and above their "dead body." This and many similar studies suggest that the brain is a kind of receiver for consciousness and memory that is being "beamed in from the Field."

Once we can accept this reality, that energy flows within us and without and we are all connected, it follows that: every thought and action is energy, therefore will affect each and every one of us, as well as the planet. Therefore we can start to take responsibility for what we think and do.

Exercises for Feeling the Energy

1. Sit comfortably and relax your shoulders and arms.

2. Hold out your palms in front of you so they are facing each other, about 2 to 3 inches apart.

3. Very slowly start pulling them away from each other until about 8 to 10 inches apart and then close together again gently.

4. Repeat several times, and you will start to feel a heaviness, or stickiness between the hands. What you feel is energy.

5. Another method is when outside, as this is easier to see, gently gaze in a relaxed manner above and you may see the energy pulsating, looking like specks of sparkly diamonds.

Human Energy Field

The human energy field or Aura, is a field of energy which surrounds and penetrates the body, is consciousness and interconnects all things and all matter. It makes up the unique spiritual, mental, emotional and physical aspects of an individual, being a template for the physical body. Disease or dis-ease will first show up in the energy field before it manifests in the physical body. Many healers work with this energy field to maintain optimum health.

Ground breaking research has been carried out by Dr Valerie Hunt, scientist and author, best known for her pioneering work in Bioenergy. She was the first to develop protocols and instrumentation necessary to detect and record the body's high frequency energy field. She discovered neuromuscular patterns of non-verbal communication showing the relationship between energy field disturbances, disease, emotional pathologies, human field communication and the energy spectrum of consciousness. Her latest work is titled, *"Uncork Your Consciousness."*

Many people are sensitive to these energy fields. Those who practise clairvoyance can see the energy with all its beautiful colours, clairsentients sense it and clairaudients will hear the energy. We all have the ability to tune into this field of energy. It is just being aware of the ability and then exercising it.

Through Kirlian Photography, which provides photographic, video or computer images of energy flow, it is now possible to see the human energy field. Household plants have been photographed in this way, and you can see a glow around the leaf which is its aura. D.R. Milner and E.F. Smart experimenting with DC high voltage photography, found there is energy transfer interaction between a freshly picked leaf and one that is dying.

I was very honoured to meet Dr Harry Oldfield, a scientist, inventor and a Fellow of the Royal Microscopical Society, Oxford, in September 2011, who was an early pioneer in the world of Kirlian Photography. His work with energy fields has opened the door to much wider fields of research and broached the previously undocumented and unfathomable: the afterlife and the space time continuum.

He went on to develop Polycontrast Interference Photography (PIP) in the 1980s. PIP can distinguish between many different grades or qualities of light and shows variations in energy fields, depicting leaks and blocks in the energy flow.

In certain circumstances the PIP technology is able to pinpoint disturbed energy states before they become evident by standard diagnosis, allowing practitioners and healers the chance to nip problems in the bud. It was developed to help improve health but it became apparent that it could also be used for investigating paranormal phenomena. With it you can see pulsating bands of energy and light, as well as graphical represented vortexes of energy, similar to the chakras described in Ayurvedic medicine and the energy meridian pathways in traditional Chinese medicine.

He showed photographs of amputees and the presence of the energy field corresponding to the missing limb could be seen. This explains on many occasions why someone who has lost a limb, can feel it, as if it is still there. What they are aware of is the energy field of the limb. For further information on Dr Harry Oldfield, refer to his website www.electrocrystal.com

William A. Tiller PhD of Stanford University states that every substance and organism radiates and absorbs energy via a unique wavefield, then exhibits certain geometrical frequencies and radiation characteristics. There is a measurable extended forcefield that exists around all forms of matter, whether animate or inanimate. A piece of jewellery for example, will have the energy of the person who made it or wore it.

Try holding a piece of jewellery in your hand that belonged to someone else. Close your eyes, and relax, allowing your thinking mind to get out of the way. This is like being in a meditative state, so see what feelings, emotions and pictures come through. Sometimes there may be a feeling of happiness if the person who wore it was jolly or sadness if they were a depressed person.

Practise at first with something from someone you know to get clarification, then maybe someone you don't know. This can be done with any significant object that belongs to someone else. Just tune into it.

If you struggle, ask your subconscious mind to help you tune in for information connected to the object.

This is a good exercise to develop intuition, and to start to learn how to listen to your inner voice.

One simple way to start seeing an aura is to go for a walk in woodland on a clear day, or just when it's starting to get dark. Then shift your gaze to the top of the trees against the sky. It may take a bit of practice, but you should see a green or grey haze around the treetop. This is the tree's auric or energy field.

You can try this with people. Allow someone to stand against a white or cream wall, removing any distractions such as pictures. Stand at least eight feet away or whatever feels right, and just allow your eyes to relax and with a glazed look, focus around the middle of the person's forehead.

Don't try too hard, relax, allowing your gaze to rest on this area. Gradually you will see a one to two inch glow around the person's head. If you are British and a certain age you may remember the old Ready Brek advert, which seemed to demonstrate this effect!

Again this may need practice, as you may not always be in the right frame of mind to do this.

Some people report seeing colours which can represent generally what is going on in the subject's life. There is nothing new about this work. We were born to live in the present moment doing whatever needed to be done, listening to our inner voice and communicating intuitively from the heart.

Nowadays we have forgotten these abilities and many of us operate through the ego, influenced by material objects. All we are aiming to do is to re-learn what we used to know how to do instinctively.

My first experience of seeing colour was around twenty years ago when I qualified as a reflexologist. As students we learned by practising on each other. I used to visit my practice partner at home and on one occasion she opened the door to me just after a quarrel with her ex-husband. I thought nothing about it and we began with her giving me a treatment.

As I was sitting there I could see a glow of red light coming out of her arm and hand. I was so excited at the time, but later felt the impact of what I had experienced. I went home, didn't sleep at all, and felt dreadful for the next three days. The red energy I saw along her arm was the anger and frustration she felt for her ex-husband coming out and being passed onto me!

This is no judgement on her, but I was grateful for this learning experience. It gave me an understanding of how unconsciously this interchange of energy can happen and, if you do not protect yourself adequately you can pick up anything that is flying around! I would urge you to be discerning with the people who come into your life.

Put simply, we all know the feeling when we have been in the company of someone who is quite negative. We go home and feel absolutely drained, or on the other hand, others who are happy, jolly and make us laugh are a tonic to be around. The message here is to try to surround yourself with positive people and protect yourself from the negative ones very well.

Laughter raises our vibration.

When a baby is born there is a strong energy connection between mother and child. This is at its strongest at birth, as they are encased in their mother's auric field. This remains the case until around the age of twelve or thirteen, when they start to create their own aura. Children often start to act independently in many ways at this age as they are starting to make their own life.

There is a vertical flow of energy that pulsates up and down the spinal cord, extending above the head and below the coccyx. Along this spinal column are seven main chakras, which correspond to a layer of the aura.

Chakras

Chakra is a Hindu word meaning "wheel." Chakras are vortexes of swirling energy, situated at the front and rear of the body, as shown in the diagram (Fig 1). Traditionally it is said we have seven primary chakras and many secondary ones, but I am focusing on the traditional seven. These are energy centres that correspond to the major nerve plexuses of the physical body in that area of the body.

They are located within the physical body, just in front of the spine, (although there are many slight variations on this). They are at the front as well as back of the body and aligned vertically up and down the spine. The universal energy flows freely through these centres, our spine, and throughout our nervous system, giving a feeling of peace and well being. Our chakra system reacts to our emotional, spiritual, mental and physical being, therefore if we are continually negative and suppress our emotions there will be blockages within these areas, which can eventually lead to disease in the corresponding area.

Seven Primary Chakras as follows:

First: Base chakra, located at the base of the spine, colour is red, and related to grounding you in the physical world. If out of balance you may sense a feeling of being a bit "airy fairy" or not belonging. Depression, lower digestive problems and gynaecological problems, can all be related to this centre.

Second: Sacral Chakra is just above the pubic bone and is orange in colour. In balance you feel very creative but if out of balance can cause reproductive issues. This is often an area where we hold childhood issues, anger and trauma.

Third: Solar Plexus is just above the navel, colour is yellow, and is the point of personal power. If out of balance can mean we become weak and fearful, angry and other extremes of emotion.

Fourth: Heart Chakra, can be a combination of pink or green, and over the heart area. This area deals with love and compassion for ourselves and others. Through it flows the energy of connectedness with all life. The more open this becomes, the more we can give and receive love. If out of balance we may lack compassion or be unable to love the self or others.

Fifth: Throat chakra is blue and over the throat area. This is the centre of good communication but if out of balance can mean we lose the ability to express ourselves clearly. We need to release and let go of judgement, criticism and anger.

Sixth: Brow or third eye chakra, is indigo, and located between the eyebrows. Often called the psychic centre, this is related to idealism and imagination. If out of balance can cause insomnia, headaches or disturbed sleep.

Seventh: Crown Chakra is violet and located at the top of the head and is the connection to the higher self, spirituality and god. When clear we are in harmony with ourselves and others, but if out of balance can cause nightmares, obsessions and general feeling of disconnectedness.

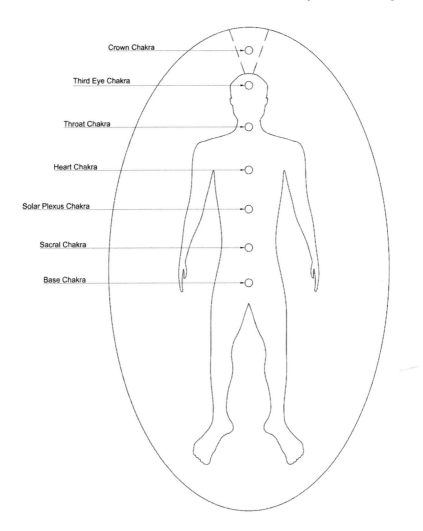

Crown Chakra

Third Eye Chakra

Throat Chakra

Heart Chakra

Solar Plexus Chakra

Sacral Chakra

Base Chakra

Always remember disease is a time to evolve, usually a "wake up call," to say you are not going with the flow of life. Stop, listen to your body and follow your heart. I have included a simple chakra meditation which you can do quickly if feeling unbalanced.

Meditation is simply being focused on something in the moment. You do not necessarily have to sit crossed legged but it is helpful to sit upright, so the energy can flow up and down the spine. Some people are unable to sit for any length of time, so remember you can meditate whilst walking, as long as you look at everything you see and not daydream about what to have for dinner! It is about being in the present moment.

Simple Chakra Mediation

We need to keep our thoughts positive and loving from the heart to ensure our chakras stay balanced. If you can't visualise in the way I suggest in the following exercise do not worry, as it is the **intent** to rebalance your chakras that carries the power.

1. Sit quietly in a comfortable chair, spine upright, feet flat on the floor.

2. Close the eyes and take a few deep breaths, releasing any tensions of the day on the out breath.

3. Visualise roots coming from your feet going deep into the earth This will ground and connect you. Allow the healing energy from the earth to rise from your feet, up to the base chakra.

4. Bring your attention to the base chakra. Allow it to be a vortex of swirling bright red light going clockwise in front of the body.

5. Then move up to the sacral chakra, (located about three fingers below the naval), imagining this as a vortex of swirling orange.

6. Move to the solar plexus, (about three fingers above the navel). Visualise the colour yellow filling this chakra and swirling out.

7. Then up to the heart chakra, between the breastbone, the colour is green, or can be a mixture of green and

pink. Repeat as above. Do this as long as it takes until you can feel the colours as vibrant swirling vortexes of healing energy.

8. Go to the throat chakra, located at the centre of the throat which is blue and repeat as above.

9. Up to the brow chakra which is indigo and repeat as above.

10. Finally to the crown chakra at the top of the head and visualise a beautiful violet light spiralling clockwise, connecting to the universe above.

11. Then flood the body with a golden light coming from the top of the head all the way down to the feet. Allow this light to expand out into the auric field (about three feet away), forming a golden egg shape around the body.

12. Visualise a golden reflective light around this egg shape, with the intention that it keeps out any non-beneficial energy.

Protection and Rebalancing Energy

There are many, many ways to clear and protect your energy. I prefer the simplest method. Some people say you do not have to do this, but I have to disagree. I have come across so many people who are depressed and after healing, the changes to their persona are tangible. Dr Alan Sanderson, is a consultant psychiatrist, hypnotherapist and spirit release therapist who discovered psychiatric patients generally had a very open or damaged auric field.

As a result detrimental energies could attach to their energy field causing them serious mental problems. If you are one of the few "enlightened" beings on this planet then maybe you don't need to protect yourself but for the rest of us, it will definitely change how

Sandra Kendrew

you feel. You can only try this for yourself! We all know the feeling when we have been with a negative depressing person, we literally feel drained. They have actually depleted our energy field, so we need to protect ourselves!

Being in nature clears your energy automatically. How many times have you gone for a walk in woodlands or open countryside, come home and felt so much better? The Chi or prana in nature cleanses energy leaving you feeling refreshed and vibrant. If you have had a bad day, or been in a negative place, or with negative people who have drained you, then I suggest taking a cold shower. I can see you curling up at the thought but give it a go. Do this for seven seconds then you are allowed to turn up the heat! Mike Robinson, author of "The True Dynamics of Life," says:

"As you move throughout the day, meeting people, or visiting places, you will be unconsciously collecting and exchanging energy. The atoms within you are magnetic, giving you an energy field which draws positive particles to it, rejecting negative particles, so by the end of the day you will have collected energy which has nothing to do with you. One of the quickest ways to deal with this energy is to have a cold shower, as cold water is also magnetic, and it draws towards it the positively charged particles that you have collected. Putting the body under cold water can release this collected energy, which otherwise over time could become detrimental to your health. Scientists have now proven the benefits of taking a cold shower twice a day, once in the morning to clear the energy from sleep, and in the evening to clear energy built up over the day"

I strongly recommend trying the following exercise morning and night for a few days, and see if your energy lifts. First thing in the morning shake your whole body. Start at the head, then shoulders, each arm, torso, right leg, then left leg. This helps move the energy and is energising. Then have your cold showers.

I use the following method for rebalancing and protecting my energy as follows:

Protection and Rebalancing Energy

Ideally done outside but if not convenient, indoors is fine:

1. Take a deep breath in, and on the out breath imagine all the non beneficial energy you have within your body is drawn from the top of the head, down through the body and out through the feet, deep into the earth to be transmuted. Do this a few times until you feel you have eliminated all your stress.

2. Then visualise a ball of golden divine healing light above the top of your head and allow this light to come down into your crown chakra at the top of your head, down the body filling it with golden healing light.

3. Once the whole body is filled with light allow this to expand out into the auric field, (about three feet all the way round), so you are forming an oval egg shape.

4. Once this protection feels strong, visualise a golden reflective light around this egg shape, with the intention it is protecting your energy and reflecting any non beneficial energies throughout day and night.

5. Do this in the morning at the start of the day, like brushing your teeth, and at night before going to bed.

Walking barefoot, as often as you can, will ground you and connect you to the energies of the earth, boost your immune system and thus cleanse your body. Do this inside and outside as often as possible. When this is impractical, choose shoes with breathable natural soles, such as leather or hide.

In conclusion, remember fear will attract more detrimental energy into your energy field. Once you have protected yourself you need to trust that this has been done. Doubt can negate and undo what you have created.

Laughter is also one of the best ways of keeping the energy clear, and will raise your consciousness or vibration. It allows the spirit to come in. We all know when people are happy we want to be in their company, because they also make us feel good!

Clearing Clutter

One great way of lightening your energy is to clear the clutter from your life. Clutter harbours negative energy. It is amazing how having a good clear out of overstuffed cupboards can improve how we feel inside.

AS WITHIN, SO WITHOUT!

Start with a small area initially and don't overface yourself, otherwise nothing will get done. Set yourself a goal, and a realistic timescale to achieve it, and write it down with intent. For example, you are going to clear your wardrobe. If we actually write out what we want to happen, it will happen. Imagine the architect preparing the plans of a building for construction. If he keeps his ideas in his head nothing will progress to reality. Here is an example:

Goal Clear my bedroom
Target One month
Action Spend two hours a week

This is just a simple suggestion, and remember the motto:

"Use it, love it or get rid of it."

Once you have started this clearing process it will become easier. If you find it really difficult to let go of your old possessions, look at what are you holding onto in your life. What emotions can't you let go of?

I have known people who have gone to a refuse tip but couldn't bear to leave their belongings, so put them back in their car and returned home. What are you hanging onto in your life? What do you fear if you let go? The Emotional Transformation Process in Chapter 3 is designed to help with this issue.

Chapter 2

Who Are We?

The Field/Creator/Source/God/Love/Universal Energy/Intelligence.

Before I go any further I want to clarify my interpretation of the above. Eckhart Tolle uses the word *Being*.

"Being is not only beyond but also deep within every form as invisible and indestructible essence. It is accessible to you now as your own deepest self, your true nature. You can know it only when the mind is still, you are present in the now. The word Being has an open concept, whereas God, creates a mental image, different for everyone, and usually something outside you."

We and everything around us are consciousness. We are all an aspect of the creator/source/God whatever word you wish to use and therefore all connected on some level.

I am going to use the word *Intelligence* for now, so I am not repeating myself many times. You can substitute the word for love, Christ, Mohammed, creator, source, universal energy, life force, field, or anything else you feel comfortable with. The intelligence we talked about earlier that flows within us and around us, and carries on into the vast universe, is the divine healing energy. It is pure unconditional love. It is the energy that healers harness and direct to whoever or whatever they are healing.

Some people think of God as a bearded man in the sky that we can never reach. God is within us and without. God is all that is. Buddha once said to a very humble man:

"Man in the street: Buddha is it true you are god

Buddha: Yes it is and so are you"

Our brain limits us in understanding who God, Buddha, Mohammed or Christ are. They are Love.

We have forgotten our ability to look inside, listen and communicate with our inner being. This is how man used to survive. He would listen to his intuition, that voice inside and act upon it in the moment. We have a world within which reflects the world outside. When we learn to listen and reconnect with our inner world, we begin to understand our greatness.

We then stop **believing** in God. We **are** God. Carl Jung, the Swiss psychiatrist and philosopher, was once asked:

"Do you believe in God?" He replied, *"No I don't believe in God, I Know God."*

If you have never tasted honey you can only say you believe honey is good. When you have **tasted** honey, you **know** honey is good! We are all a divine spark of the creator, making us also creators of our own life. Those who have forgotten to do that are not living to their full potential. Now is the time to pick yourself up and enjoy the ride!

What affects one person affects another. Look inside and scan your body. Where are you holding onto the anger, guilt, and fear? We are all living stressful lives, worrying about the past, what the future holds, so no wonder the whole world seems chaotic! It is being affected by all our stress. We can do something about it now by starting to look at ourselves.

We are All Connected

Ed Mitchell, a member of the Apollo 12 crew and the sixth man to land on the moon made some fascinating observations. Journalist

Lynne McTaggart interviewed him and recounts in her book, "The Field":

"It was then, while staring out of the window, that Ed experienced the strangest feeling he would ever have: a feeling of connectedness, as if all the planets and all the people of all times were attached in some visible web. He could hardly breathe because of the majesty of the moment. Although he continued to turn knobs, and press buttons, he felt distanced from his body, as though someone else was doing the navigating.

There seemed to be an enormous force field here, connecting all people, their intentions and thoughts, and every animate and inanimate form of matter for all time. Time was just an artificial construct"

Basically there is no separation between each and every one of us and the universe. We are all connected at some level. Every person's thoughts and actions affect each and everyone one of us. We all need to be more responsible for how we act. If individually we started to live a life with pure thought, compassion and love, we would affect everyone around us, ultimately creating a more peaceful, harmonious planet.

Think of a tree, it takes in carbon dioxide and gives out oxygen. We breathe in the oxygen and breathe out the carbon dioxide, and the flow goes on. The universal life force, this field, or sea of energy flows through and out of us and connects us all.

Spirituality and Religion

Being "spiritual" is not about what you believe but everything to do with raising your consciousness and living your life, from the heart. Then comes an awakening and understanding.

As mentioned earlier, the consciousness of people and the planet is increasing quite dramatically, as we are becoming more heart centred and less materialistic. Some of the religious institutions will be open to the new consciousness and work from a place of love and empathy, whilst others will harden their doctrinal positions and increase the control and power they have over people.

Spiritual seekers tend to think, "One day I will find enlightenment." This suggests a time in the future, possibly years ahead, but if we realise we don't need time to be who we are, it can happen right now. Just let go and surrender.

As Eckhart Tolle in "A New Earth" says:

"Heaven is not a location, but refers to the inner realm of consciousness. A new heaven is the emergence of a transformed state of human consciousness, and a new earth, is its reflection in the physical realm"

When we start to work on ourselves and balance mind, spirit and body, we start to know and feel the peace of our soul. We can then bring heaven to earth!

We have all lost our way, with years of illusion. God does not punish or judge. How can love punish?

When we become realigned, we have truth and freedom. To be free and get reconnected to the universal energy of pure love is to go within and purify our thoughts, words and actions. When we do this and have a clear space this universal energy can enter our being. Once we start to live in the present moment, in our *beingness*, in other words simply *just are*, then we can live in a world free of fear and manifest the life we choose.

Reincarnation

The Bhagavad-gita, a seven hundred verse Hindu scripture, is one of the most important texts in the history of literature and philosophy and explains that whatever state of consciousness we attain in this life, through our thoughts, actions and deeds, will determine what happens in the next life. It is the rebirth of a soul in a new body and the body chosen will assist the soul in evolving and learning whatever it needs to know and experience.

This may be a difficult concept to grasp but we all choose our parents! We select the parents that will help us with the important lessons we have to learn. We choose parents who will teach us what we need to know to balance out the Karma. For example, someone who in a previous life was a doctor who abused his position of trust may return to this earth as a doctor again, but one with true compassion and empathy for human suffering and pain. This is the Earth School, a place of learning, to free ourselves from emotional burdens, to find truth and freedom.

When we reincarnate, a veil is put over our memory from past lives, otherwise we wouldn't learn. There are many people who have experienced the sensation of "déjà vu" when something or someone is familiar. These feelings may be flashbacks to those previous, hidden memories.

When we realise we choose our life, family and friends for our own learning it helps us to be less judgemental. If someone annoys us it is useful to think they were chosen so that we experience and learn from that emotion. What an empowering and liberating concept! The people that are placed in our life to "push our buttons" are actually helping us to release emotions from the subconscious mind, although most of us aren't aware this is happening. How we deal with this is explained in the chapter on Emotional Transformation.

Your Soul and Karma

Human beings may be highly intelligent, very advanced both technically and scientifically, but their connection to spirituality is zero! Worshipping the intellectual mind carries a downside as we have lost touch with our intuition and our real intelligence. Many people are starting to awaken and realise that we are mind, body and soul, and know there is something much bigger than just this physical body we have.

Eckhart Tolle, author of "A New Earth" explains Karma:

"Re-birth or reincarnation is of course part of karma, but if you do not believe in this you can look at re-birth in your own life. Every time you identify with a thought that arises, you are born into that thought. Your identity, your sense of self is in it. That's karma. Your karma is the identification with these patterns that you have inherited-the conditioned.

Karma is the complete absence of conscious Presence. It is automatic. It plays itself out. The only thing that can free you of karma is the arising of Presence. It can happen at any time, it can happen to a criminal in prison, it can happen to someone who has never heard of anything spiritual, it can happen to someone who has been meditating for thirty years. Time does not free you of karma"

Presence frees you from karma, the old thought patterns may pop up but will not have an effect on you. There are many spiritual teachers who are here now to help with this process of awakening, or releasing karma. If you find you are on this pathway of awakening you will be a natural teacher, there to guide others on their journey.

You need to get out of the ego, and allow the intelligence to flow through. This will not happen if you are caught up in the mind.

People will be drawn to you and your consciousness may respond by saying something that you didn't know you knew the answer to. Act now and stay present to free yourself.

We have come to the earth to allow our souls to evolve through life's experiences, to spiritualise nature, and whatever pathway we choose, ultimately our goal is to raise our consciousness.

Dr Wayne W. Dyer internationally renowned author and speaker says:

"We are not human beings having a spiritual experience. We are spiritual beings having a human experience"

Claire Montanaro, author of "Spiritual Wisdom" also says:

"Everything you do, say, think affects your ability to progress as a spiritual being. It impacts your work, your relationships, your health, your finances, your overall well-being-the whole of your life and every part of your life, at all levels. This is Karma, the Universal Law of Cause and Effect."

It is the totality of all your previous thoughts, words and actions that will affect your present reality. Whatever you put out, you will get back! If you do an act of kindness, this will raise your consciousness, allowing you to become more evolved. Karma is never a punishment, it is rebalancing whatever you have done. For example, if some one had spent a life in a state of envy and greed that led them to steal from others, they may, at a later stage, have to learn what it is to live in a state of poverty or be in a position where they can balance out their karma by giving away their wealth to those who have nothing.

As Dr Deepak Chopra, a world renowned authority in the field of mind-body healing, and best selling author, says on his website:

" Karma is a conditioned response, most people are operating under the bondage of karma, the past influences the present. Every action generates a force of energy that returns to us in like kind-what we sow is what we reap"

The aim in this life is to be free of karma, stay present, then, we will have infinite creativity and inspiration, able to manifest whatever we wish for, as long as it is for our highest good!

The soul is formless, non physical energy and each time it incarnates on the earth it is here to learn and improve.

The soul will have chosen when to pass over before it incarnates. When it is the right time the soul will leave the body. This is difficult for those around the dying person as they may feel they no longer exist. It is an illusion to think death is the end because on the other side it is just the beginning! Einstein said:

"Energy cannot be created or destroyed"

When we think about our loved ones, we will be energetically connected to them. Where our thoughts are, our energy goes. One of the hardest and most sensitive losses to understand is a miscarriage or a termination of pregnancy. It can be a great comfort to the mother to know that it was pre-ordained that this soul should come into her life for a short time, and that she is helping it to move on by letting go. This is usually a karmic agreement between the parents and soul of a child before it decides to reincarnate.

Human Conditioning

I liken the mind to a computer, collecting knowledge from the past and storing it to use for the present moment.

From birth until the present, our personality is made up of our belief system, what we like and dislike, our fears, competitiveness, the way we behave and express ourselves. Beliefs are thoughts we have as children and grow up believing them to be the case. This becomes our conditioning and part of our subconscious mind.

Conditioning usually goes deep into the subconscious mind. If a child grows up with parents whose love is unconditional, and the child experiences acts of love, this is recorded in the subconscious mind, and therefore a positive act of human conditioning.

If on the other hand a child has been scared by a dog and didn't process this fear in the conscious mind, it will embed itself in the subconscious. The child will inevitably grow up fearful of dogs for life.

Conditioning comes from family, teachers, peers, the media, in short, the sum total of life experiences. The Key to freeing yourself, is being conscious and present in your daily life. It takes some practice, but a few breaths will always bring you back into the present moment. Keep practising and focus on the now, not past or future.

Start to be who you really are. I am going to suggest a simple daily meditation to bring you into your body, in the present, and calm the mind from the busy everyday clutter so that you can get to know the real you. I suggest you just concentrate on the in and out breath. If any thoughts come into your mind, don't judge, allow them to float out again, and keep focused on the breath. It is helpful to keep a daily journal of thoughts that come in during the meditation and at other times during the day, or through dreams.

If it is comfortable try to breathe through the nose during the meditation but if difficult then use the mouth.

Simple Meditation

1. Sit with your spine upright on a comfortable chair, feet firmly on the ground. Close your eyes and imagine roots from your feet going deep into the earth, to help ground you.

2. Take three really deep breaths and relax, allowing any tensions from the top of your head down to your feet to float into the earth.

3. If your shoulders are tense, lift them up to your ears, roll back and release down. Repeat three times.

4. Breathe into the body feeling the abdomen expanding on the in breath, and contracting on the out breath.

5. If you wish you can imagine yourself surrounded by light, allowing it to gradually fill the whole body, so you are completely immersed in a sea of luminous light.

6. You can now focus on feelings within the body. See what emotion lies underneath the feeling. If nothing comes up go deeper, just accepting and observing.

7. Do this for twenty minutes ideally morning and night, but do whatever you can without putting pressure on yourself.

8. At the end just sit and enjoy the moment.

9. This is a time you can always ask the universe or higher self for advice or answers, or simply connect to your inner being. This will help raise your consciousness as you are being present.

Whilst you are doing your meditation, who is watching the thoughts you have?

One exercise I learnt from Claire Montanaro, author of *"Spiritual Wisdom,"* is Being Who You Are. Most of us are conditioned to impress others by what we wear and how we look. We can hide behind these masks and not be recognised for who we are. There is a requirement in many communities to conform, and whilst some people like to feel "one of the crowd," others will rebel.

Being Who You Are

Start by looking in the mirror. Look at your hair, and gradually work your way down, from the clothes you are wearing, your face and make-up, if you wear it, to your shoes. How do you feel about yourself? Have you had the same hairstyle since you were a teenager? Is your make-up a bit dowdy?

Maybe a simple change in the colours you wear could lift your spirits. We can all get into ruts, lazy and fearful of making changes. Look through your wardrobe, and if you haven't already, clear out all those old items that you never wear.

Are you a person who hides behind dark colours? Even if you like black, maybe a pink shirt or blouse will make you feel brighter. At the start of the day ask yourself what colours would make you feel good. Don't forget you have choice. Your clothes represent you and how you feel about yourself.

How do you see yourself? Write down your personality traits, good and bad. Are you aggressive, bossy, compassionate, calm, intellectual, articulate, shy or something else? Try to identify the type of person or archetype you are.

We are human, so don't judge or criticise yourself. Acceptance is the key. In your journal write down how often you judge or criticise yourself and others. By being aware, gradually the positives will outweigh the negatives. Try to observe without judgement. Criticism feeds the ego, affects your energy, so you find yourself more in a place of darkness than light. So keep those thoughts positive and let your light shine like a star.

Be aware of your body and be grateful for your body, for all the infinite intelligence that exists within it and the wonderful job it does in keeping you alive and protected. Remember before acting on any emotion, the ego will want to answer first, but go into the heart for the truthful answer. Whenever you have a difficult decision to make just sit quietly, go into your heart area and go with the first answer it gives you.

Imagine you have been offered two jobs and you don't know which one to take. Try not to get into the mind, as it could come back and say, "but the other job pays better." We don't always know the bigger picture, so trust your intuition to point to the true path and go with the flow of life. Stress, is going against the flow of life. When you become stressed, go inside and listen to the body and always follow what the heart is telling you. It knows!

Before you go to sleep, run through the day's events, as if watching a movie screen. When were you acting out of ego, and when from your heart, your true self? Ask yourself why you acted out of ego. Was it to make you look better, more important, to gain admiration or love? Start to look deeper within. Maybe there's a lack of self worth and self love within you?

Chapter 3

Subconscious and Conscious Mind

"Your Beliefs become your Thoughts
Your Thoughts become your Words
Your Words become your Actions
Your Actions become your Habits
Your Habits become your Values
Your Values become your Destiny"

Mahatma Gandi

We are the sum total of our every thought, word, belief and action.

Simply put, the conscious mind is the creative and the part that is responsible for logic and reasoning. You use your conscious mind to write, go on the internet, ride a bike, dress yourself, add up, or a voluntary movement like moving your hand or leg. If there is logic or reasoning then you are using the conscious mind. The conscious mind only operates about five per cent of the time.

The subconscious mind, on the other hand, is responsible for all your involuntary actions, such as your breathing, heart beat and emotions, in fact all we have ever learned becomes subconscious behaviour, such as driving a car. How many times have you driven a car, had a conscious conversation with your passenger and realised, when you arrived at your destination, you cannot remember any of the journey. The subconscious mind has driven you to your destination. Our subconscious mind operates about ninety five per cent of the time.

Bruce H. Lipton PhD, author of "The Biology of Belief" says:

"The conscious mind is the creative mind which represents the seat of our personality, source, or spirit. It can see into the future, review the past, or disconnect from the present moment as it solves problems in our head. In its creative capacity, the conscious mind holds our wishes, desires, and aspirations for our lives. It is the mind that conjures up our positive thoughts.

In contrast, the subconscious mind is primarily a repository of stimulus-response tapes derived from instincts and learned experiences. The subconscious mind is fundamentally habitual: it will play the same behavioural responses to life's signals over and over again, much to our chagrin. How many times have you found your self going ballistic over something trivial like an open toothpaste tube? You have been trained since childhood to replace the cap. When you find the cap left off, your "buttons are pushed," and you automatically fly into a rage. You've just experienced the simple stimulus-response of a behaviour program stored in the subconscious mind. The subconscious mind is a million more times powerful than the conscious mind. If the desires of the conscious mind conflict with the programs in the subconscious mind, which mind do you think will win?"

For those of you that do positive affirmations, (a positive statement), this may explain why they never work. If the subconscious operates ninety five per cent of the time, the conscious mind does not stand a chance. So when you look in the mirror and say, "I am worthy and confident," but as a child you were often told, "you're not good enough," then it is the latter which will win through!

You can liken a CD player to the subconscious mind. Imagine you don't like what the music is playing. If you ask it to play something else, like the subconscious mind, it takes no notice and carries on playing. The trick is to learn how to press the record button, then you can record new programmes for the subconscious mind to play.

Usually up to the age of six is the time when information regarding the child's perception of the world is absorbed by the subconscious mind.

Unconscious belief systems can destroy your life. If you believe yourself to be frail and ill, this is what you become. As Mike Robinson, author of "The True Dynamics of Life" says:

"The unconscious is your conditioning and hidden intent rising up into the conscious. If we were to observe ourselves, all that is hidden in the unconscious world would come out into the light and be consciously known. The unconscious can only remain hidden if you let it. Once you start to observe your intent, (it may be gossip about someone), all those hidden aspects become known. This is self-knowledge, and only you can do it"

Do not punish yourself for acting the way you have in the past. Show gratitude for the awakening at last!

There are many techniques which can be used as a tool to clear the patterns of the subconscious and different methods suit different people, such as:

Energy Psychology ie Emotional Freedom Technique

EFT is a powerful self help method based on the fact emotional trauma can contribute to dis-ease. Scientific studies have shown EFT is able to rapidly reduce memory incidents which trigger an emotional response. It is very easy to learn, and involves tapping on various meridians in the body. Many GPs and therapists are incorporating this method into their practice. There are many websites on this and the one I recommend is www.eftuniverse.com

I suggest after this exercise imagine your whole being flooded with white light and protected

PSYCH-K.

Short for Psychological Kinesiology, this is a simple powerful method using muscle testing to free your mind of negative subconscious beliefs that perpetuate old habits and sabotage your success and peace in life. Refer to www.psych-k.com

Hypnotherapy

A practitioner will guide a subject into a deep relaxed state creating an altered state of awareness, different from being awake or asleep. Under hypnosis a person is usually responsive to ideas, concepts and lifestyle changes. As the subconscious mind is revealed it is possible to release and re-programme patterns of limiting beliefs.

Emotional Clearing

Emotional clearing is a system of inner healing, based on a unique synthesis of ancient and modern knowledge-a combination of Eastern spiritual and Western psychological principles. It works in a state of relaxation by adjusting and aligning each of the five levels of Being-Physical, Energetic, Mental, Intellectual and Spiritual to release negative feelings and emotions and promote the true serenity of transcendental consciousness. See www.emclear.com

11 x 22s

This I learnt from Mike Robinson, author of "The True Dynamics of Relationships." This is a very powerful method of revealing and clearing the subconscious mind.

The process takes place over eleven consecutive days (otherwise you have to return to day one!), followed by eleven days off, if you need to do it again. The system involves choosing an affirmation, which is relevant, and covers an issue you may have in your life, for example if you lack confidence, maybe use a statement like, "I am perfectly acceptable and confident in all I do." This is a much deeper practice than looking in a mirror and saying "I am confident." This can take twenty minutes or two hours, so be prepared.

Write your chosen sentence out once, then immediately write down whatever comes into your mind, whether it is an agreement or disagreement with your sentence. Just keep writing until a pause, then write out the statement again, continuing to write whatever comes into your mind, even if you feel like a cup of tea, write it down, until a pause. Keep this up until you have written the sentence out twenty two times, with your response. If you reach say number eight, and nothing comes into the mind, write "nothing," and carry on with number nine.

You can have either an eleven day break or leave until a suitable time and begin the cycle again with another sentence. The intention is this process starts to clear the energy within the body and mind immediately. Occasionally you may feel like crying or hitting a pillow, allow yourself to do this, it releases the emotion. Sometimes a memory comes up, just accept, this is part of the healing process.

The idea of the 11/22s is to bring everything to the surface, releasing all blockages. We store our negative experiences, trauma and sadness within the cells, muscles, organs and joints of the body. This method alongside the cold showers helps to release this stored energy. Then visualise filling yourself with healing white light, surrounded by an orb of golden reflective light for protection.

Emotional Transformation Process

The above methods are tools to help clear the patterns of the subconscious, but ultimately if we live in the present moment, our mind cannot take over. We then live with a conscious mind. See at the end of this chapter how to benefit from this process, which I and many others have practised. It helps to eventually release old negative belief patterns. Being conscious as this process describes is the key to freedom, truth and joy.

Cross Crawl Exercise

These are exercises to re-programme the nervous and other systems within the body as well as muscle co-ordination. The left side of the brain sends information to the right side of the brain and vice versa. We have electrical impulses that pass between the two hemispheres of the brain and they need to be balanced, to allow the male and female energy to function to its optimum level.

When energy doesn't flow and becomes blocked you may experience the following symptoms:

+ Lethargy

+ Lack of co-ordination

+ Learning disabilities

+ Being unbalanced

+ Dyslexia

+ Clumsiness

+ Shallow breathing

+ Lacking in Energy

The cross crawl exercise practised daily for a few minutes can help integrate both sides of the brain. There is a programme called Educational Kinesiology which helps children with learning disabilities. More information can be found on the website at www. braingym.org

Cross Crawl

1. Stand upright and on an in breath raise and elevate the right arm above the head, at the same time raise the opposite leg bending the knee. If you are unable to stand the exercises can be performed from a seated position.

2. Re-pattern the brain by turning the head towards the raised hand, then straighten the head, breathe out as the arm and leg come down.

3. Breathe in as you raise the left arm and right knee, turning the head to look at the left hand.

4. Straighten the head as you breathe out and allow the arm and leg to come down.

5. Repeat twenty two times or as many as is comfortable.

6. Now as the knee is raised tap it with the opposite hand, repeat on the other side by raising the other knee and tap with the opposite hand. Repeat for a further twenty two times.

7. This technique is excellent for very young babies and can be performed whilst laying on the floor and bringing one foot up to touch the opposite hand.

This will improve:

* Focus and concentration
* Boost energy levels
* Improve co-ordination
* Give more confidence
* More balance in your life
* Enhanced breathing and stamina
* Good for stroke victims

Conscious Parenting

As parents we all do our very best at the time and have to accept that without self judging. The key of being a conscious parent is to give your child attention. As Eckhart Tolle, author of "A New Earth" and "The Power of Now," says:

"There are two kinds of attention, one called form based attention, the other formless attention. Form based attention is always connected with doing or evaluating, "Have you done your homework? Eat your dinner, tidy your room, hurry up, get ready." This is of course necessary to some extent. Formless attention is when you look at, listen to, touch or help your child, you are alert, still, completely present, not wanting anything but the moment as it is"

This is conscious parenting, and very valuable in a relationship with children. The first six or seven years children learn through imitation, so check your actions are worthy and not giving mixed messages. It is no good when we say one thing, and our actions say another. Be Present in every interaction with your children and view the tantrums as opportunities to reverse the negative patterns taught by your elders, or the media. Children live in the present moment and are expressing themselves in the present, therefore instead of controlling them, allow them to be with their feelings and express themselves but obviously this is not letting them do what they want.

As a general guide try to let go of unfounded fears and avoid implanting unnecessary worries and limiting beliefs in your child's subconscious mind. Most of all remember, for human beings to obtain optimum growth on their journey, is not going to the most exclusive school, living in the biggest house or having the latest and best toys. It is LOVE.

Thoughts and Feelings

It is the constant mental chatter of thoughts that prevents us from finding inner calm. We have become slaves to our minds and have become caught up in the illusion of thought, but thoughts don't hold power unless they become a belief.

Thoughts are energy and we are sending and receiving information, backwards and forwards continuously. It is like an invisible conversation but we are not aware of it. Remember all these judgements and criticisms we are thinking are energy and have to go somewhere, usually whoever we are holding a grudge against will be affected by them. This also applies to ourselves.

If we constantly judge our own behaviour and criticise ourselves this negative energy will be held within our own energy system and also attract more of the same. We all know people who seem to move from one disaster to another. They are actually attracting to them what they are thinking. To break the cycle they need to stop and take responsibility for those thoughts.

To free yourself from the mind, start watching your thoughts as often as you can. Look for repetitive patterns and be the observer with no judgement. You then enter a new dimension of consciousness, where the thought loses its power as you have stopped giving it energy. You will get more and more of these still moments with more practise, which will free you from this constant chatter. Thoughts and emotions will still come but they won't take you over. You, your higher self will be in charge!

As Lynne McTaggart, author of "The Field" says:

"We understand from science that we are not separate, that we are a part of a giant energy field, the zero point field, and when you get down to it in the lower level of our being, the undercoat of our being, even subatomic particles aren't separate things. They are packets of vibrating energy that trade energy all the time. On that level and above, things are a lot less individual than we thought they are. It's very difficult to separate out where one thing ends and another thing begins.

Another important bit of science to understand with intention, is in a sense we are all candles. We are all emitting light. A German scientist called Fritz-Albert Popp had an amazing eureka moment when he discovered all living things are emitting a tiny current of light. They are just a tiny current of bio photon emissions, as he called them, and this light is not only sent out by all living things, but picked up by all the other living things around them and responded to.

So, we're having this conversation, as mentioned earlier between all living things. We are sending and receiving. We are, in a sense, like an antenna transmitter and receiver all in the same body. Like a television set and television station all at once."

The self fulfilling prophecy is at work in parents who were not sports loving youngsters, believing this will result in their children also not liking sports. These thoughts are part of a belief system that needs to be broken. Whatever you think tends to become your reality.

It is a good idea to keep a journal and write down how many positive and negative thoughts you have during the day. You can then look at yourself, without judging of course! Once the realisation happens gradually the positive thoughts will outweigh the negative. How many times do you here someone say,

"We can't afford this, and can't afford that"
"Why does it always happen to me?"
"I don't think I will ever get a job"
"It's bad news after bad news!"
"Don't think I'll pass"
"I'm not good enough to ..."

How often are you voicing these thoughts? Remember they create our reality.

Our mind likes to tell us we are not worthy or not loved. Being an observer of our thoughts slows them down. Being detached from our emotions gradually frees us from the chaos and allows us to be the master, not the mind.

A useful exercise if you find your mind is getting too busy is to just sit quietly and take three deep breaths into the abdomen. This will focus you back into your body, allowing you to become present.

Twenty five per cent of energy in the body is used to operate the brain. When thinking you use lots of energy and if our thoughts are not of a positive manner they can be counterproductive and create a reality that we have then to overcome.

Next time you consciously have a thought, take a moment and ask yourself, has that thought enhanced my life, or taken away from my life? Be more conscious, and responsible for what goes out into the world. The more our thoughts are put into the negative aspect such as fear and worry, we not only waste energy but it impairs the immune system.

Conserve your energy to create positivity, which will lift everyone's heart.

> *Worrying Is Praying For Something That You*
> *Do Not Want. So Stop Worrying!*
> Bhagavan Das

DNA Research

A Russian Scientist Dr Vladamir Poponin discovered multi-dimensional fields around DNA, in other words DNA has a quantum field filled with information from every single lifetime. Russian biophysicist and molecular biologist Pjotr Garjajev has investigated cutting edge research, of a more esoteric nature, which explains phenomena such as intuition, remote healing and self-healing.

They found our DNA can cause disturbing patterns in the vacuum or field and how information can be transmitted outside time and space and into our consciousness. We have the potential to rewrite our DNA. More information is available on the internet regarding the research, but it proves the incredible power we have within, and we are only using around three to five per cent of it.

Dr Bruce Lipton PhD, author of "The Biology of Belief," says we can change our DNA and cells, with our emotions. By changing our belief system and human conditioning, we can change our genetic make up, and ultimately live the life we want.

Dr Masaru Emoto

I first realised how our thinking creates our reality, when I saw "What The Bleep Do We Know," taken from the website www.whatthebleep.com.

This was first released in 2004 and went on to become a successful documentary, stunning audiences with its revolutionary blend of dramatic film, documentary, animation, comedy, quantum physics, spirituality, neurology and evolutionary thought. A must to see.

It features a young girl looking at herself in a mirror, hating her appearance and repulsed by her weight. She then goes down through an underground train station and notices a display of photographs by Dr Emoto taken after his experiments during the 1990s, observing the effect of words, prayer, music and environment on the crystalline structure of water. This showed how our thoughts and feelings affect physical reality.

His research proved how concentrated positive thoughts, sent to water, produced changes that could be observed through a microscope. When focused thoughts of love and gratitude were sent to the water sample, a crystal formed, perfect and symmetrical in every way as shown below, from the "Office Masara Emoto, LLC.

41

Love and Gratitude

When thoughts of "You Make Me Sick," were focused on the water, a murky looking mass was observed as shown below.

You Make Me Sick

When water is subjected to Vivaldi's Four Seasons, it takes on the appearance of a beautiful snowflake. This proves water has memory, so respect it! His latest book, "The Hidden Messages in Water" is truly inspiring. See www.masaru-emoto.net

It needs to be remembered that humans and the planet are made up of approximately seventy five per cent water. The message here is if we send negative thoughts to our body such as "I hate the way I look," or "I am fat and ugly," imagine what these thoughts are creating within. These thoughts lower our energy or consciousness, and attract more of what we are thinking. So the girl in the underground who continually thought of herself as fat, will have created this, even more so. Energy follows thought, whatever we think we create!

Emotion

We have to accept the way we are, and Be Who We Are, then, with focused awareness, our perception can change. Fear is usually behind an emotion. A daily exercise for body awareness is beneficial, as below:

Body Awareness Exercise

1. Give your body permission to sit quietly for twenty minutes. We need to be more grateful for what our body does for us, day in and day out.

2. Take a deep breath, close your eyes, and just focus inside the body. Observe without judgement where you feel an ache or pain, anger, tension or any other emotion within the body.

3. Keep focusing, just accepting what happens is perfect, going deeper, maybe looking at the trigger of the emotion, and breathe into it. Allow the emotion to rise, staying with it until gradually it will change.

4. Sometimes a memory may be brought up, just accept, don't analyse. Repeat every time you feel stressed.

5. Before you act upon any emotion, go into your heart, this is your best guide!

6. Give your body permission to do whatever it feels, even if this is crying. The more you get to know your body the more it will heal and know what to do.

7. At the end say, "My intent is to do this body awareness daily so I become aware of what my body is telling me, and bring inner joy."

The intention is to continually do this throughout the day being aware of emotional triggers in the moment, and allowing them to flow through instead of being stuck when we don't express ourselves.

Emotion is the body's reaction to the mind. E-Motion is energy in motion, and as we are energy beings, if we do not allow this energy to flow through us in the moment, thus suppressing our emotions and feelings, it will block somewhere within the body. If not dealt with, it can turn into illness. Healers can assist in unblocking this energy, but ultimately we should do it ourselves in the moment. A good healer will show you how to do this for yourself.

This is empowering and ensures you don't come to rely on the therapist. They are there to show you the way, so you can take responsibility for yourself.

Constant negative thoughts, born out of anger and frustration will create a build up of energy in the body and if held onto for a long period will affect the biochemistry of the body.

Energy flows into the body through the top of the head and is processed at different locations throughout the body, like food is processed in different organs, then flows out again. If we are detached from our emotions and simply observe, the energy will flow freely through the body, but if we become caught up in them, fear will creep in and our energy will become stuck. Anger, grief, jealousy, sadness and loneliness are all fear-based emotions. These emotions come from our energy system, and no one or thing is to blame.

Every emotion we get is a message from our soul, so instead of reacting with anger, resentment or fear, start to listen to the body, and if you don't listen the same message/emotion will resurface again and again. How many times have you had a situation repeat itself? This is *you* not listening! No-one can help you listen to your body. It is your job to focus inside.

One major wake up call for me was the realisation that people come into our lives to help us on our pathway. People mirror us! Once we realise this, it can help to loosen those feelings of hate and anger that take hold. When someone *presses your buttons*, or simply annoys you, it is your feelings which are being brought to the surface-they are simply the trigger.

Once you are aware of this, next time, instead of reacting, just accept the feeling, breathe into it and release in the moment. Don't punish yourself if you do react and hurl abuse at someone, but when you find a quiet moment try the Emotional Transformational Process given further on.

Accepting that people and situations are doing us a great favour by "pressing our buttons," is the first step, as it is helping us to recognise we have this stuck emotion in our energy system that needs releasing! When you start to practise how to respond to these emotions instead of suppressing them, they can be dealt with in the moment and released. Just start to watch where in the body you hold onto this feeling when someone upsets you. Challenge the fear by not acting on it, breathe into the feeling and let go. Once mastered, this creates a shift in energy. Many people become their emotions and suffer panic, resulting in an overactive mind that never finds peace.

Picture yourself sitting on a riverbank, watching the flow of the water. The river represents your thoughts and emotions. Stay detached and watch them float by. Don't let your emotions and thoughts pull you into the river and carry you away!

> *"A human being is part of the whole, called by us "Universe", a part limited in time and space. He experiences himself, his thoughts, and feelings as something separated from the rest, a kind of optical delusion of his consciousness. This delusion is a kind of prison for us, restricting us to our personal desires and to affection for a few persons nearest to us. Our task must be to free ourselves from this prison by widening our circle of compassion to embrace all living creatures and the whole of nature in its beauty. Nobody is able to achieve this completely, but the striving for such achievement is in itself a part of the liberation and a foundation for inner security."*
>
> Albert Einstein

How to deal with emotions

- When a negative feeling comes up, be aware of what is happening but don't become involved

- Don't react, judge or blame anyone else. This is your feeling, no-one else's, so own the feeling

- Locate in the body where you feel this emotion and breathe into that area. Get to know your body, it will heal itself.

The following meditation called **Emotional Transformation Process** can be used to release emotions, and help disease, aches, tensions and pain in the body. A simpler version in Chapter 4, called *Simple Mindfulness Exercise* can be used quickly if you haven't much time. Eventually you will be able to act in the moment, and process any feelings or emotions which arise-but deal with them, otherwise they become suppressed and lead to physical illness.

Emotional Transformation Process

The cause of all illness is emotion!

1. Take three deep breaths, protect and ground yourself. Allow about twenty minutes to do the exercise.

2. Tap firmly in the thymus area, (between the chest and neck area) with the fist for a couple of minutes, to boost the immune system and calm you down. Can be done any time as a quick stress release, breathing and letting go.

3. Set an intention ie "My intention is to release any blocks that stop me living fully in the present moment, in peace, joy and love." Really feel the whole body is in a completely relaxed state.

4. Now go into the body, feel any pain, tension, and emotions that are causing distress, realising no-one is to blame, this is your feeling or pain, so instead of reacting, let go of any situation or person's behaviour that may have triggered it.

5. Accept any feelings or pain you have, just watch and observe for a few minutes or as long as it feels comfortable, really feel the emotion or pain, but stay detached, view as the witness, and don't analyse. Keep breathing and let go.

6. Focusing on the emotions allow the energy and cells to change. Get to know your inner body. It will heal itself! Keep breathing! This is processing the emotions, and gradually you will be able to do this in the moment when a negative feeling is brought up, or an ache or pain.

7. Once we become conscious of our emotions and pain within, gradually the energy from this will dissipate, and we will realise that is all it is-energy. Sometimes

people or situations may come flooding into the mind, just observe whatever happens is perfect, and if nothing happens, that is also fine.

8. The mind is not you, it feeds the emotions, causing distress, but look at this as a ball of energy from your past beliefs, still lingering around you, and focusing in a detached way will shrink it. Accept this and you will start to feel better.

9. Every so often when appropriate, take a deep breath and release.

10. If you feel tearful, it is fine to cry, or shout as this is a release of the emotion, so don't suppress it. Completely surrender to the feeling.

11. When you have finished visualise yourself and aura full of light, surrounded by a golden egg shape of reflective light around you, about three feet in diameter, protecting your energy.

12. Keep practising until gradually your ache, pain or emotion dissipates, and your "buttons are not pressed."

13. The aim is to be able to deal with these feelings and emotions in the moment. You may still have your "buttons pushed" but it will be more conscious than unconscious.

14. See the issue, accept it and process it. This technique is a tool to bring awareness to the pain body, which has possibly been with you since childhood.

15. Most of us suppress our emotions by keeping busy but we must deal with them. If we keep resisting the feeling they will get stronger, and prevent us finding inner peace, love and joy in our lives!

16. Eventually at regular intervals scan the body, how does it feel? How's your emotions? How's the mind? The mind creates emotions, which affect you physically! Accept without judgement this is how it is, don't analyse, breathe deeply, and focus on the present moment.

If you find difficulty on focusing on the breath, and your mind wanders, repeat on the in breath "in" and on the out breath "out." This will focus the mind, then, when in a state of calm just allow yourself to be.

Remember at any time, if you find yourself with a busy mind, caught up in the past or future, bring yourself back into the present moment by breathing in three times,

To further the practice if you wish, whilst breathing, focus at the third eye centre, (the area between the eyebrows) as this helps raise the consciousness.

Chapter 4

Fear and Love

Anger

Anger often happens when we do not speak our truth in the moment. Those who express how they feel, at the time, will most likely succeed in clearing the air. What sometimes happens is they express themselves, then apologize, taking it all back, so it re-manifests in the next argument. When we hold onto anger, we may find small things annoy and irritate us, so if we don't express ourselves, this will be stored until someone triggers something, then a person in the line of fire will be the receiver of their fury!

Later in life this unexpressed anger will be held somewhere in the energy system, and may eventually become the root cause of an illness. Even if an illness occurs, which will have underlying emotion, use the Emotional Transformation Process.

Anger and frustrations can build up in the body. Consider this scenario. You are waiting to pay in the supermarket and someone pushes in front of you. Instead of saying in a calm assertive voice in the moment, "Excuse me but I think I am in front of you," you may choose to say nothing but keep your fury inside, unexpressed. Later you may find the pent up anger is released onto someone undeserving, whereas if you had spoken to the person who jumped the queue in the first place, the anger would not have accumulated.

Anger has its roots in fear, usually fear of not being loved. We may become frightened to voice our true feelings because we fear disapproval. When anger rises try not to label the emotion, stay detached, observe it, and then it will change.

Another way of dealing with this hidden anger is to write a letter to whoever you feel is causing you this pain. Empty all your feelings out onto paper. When you feel calm then destroy the letter, with love. With practise you will be able to do this in the moment when the situation arises. Anger reflects a lack of self worth, a feeling you are not in control or not good enough.

Grief

This is a difficult emotion. There is nothing wrong with grieving, but if it has not been sufficiently expressed, it can be the cause of physical symptoms. Don't punish yourself for whatever has happened, no-one is to blame, just accept whatever it is, move away from the past by accepting, forgiving, with no blame and try to move into the present. Grief is a way of preparing us for new beginnings. The karma is finished, so it is time to let go.

Loss of a Loved One

This is possibly one of our hardest challenges, the greatest fear in life and very difficult to explain. All our fears, if we peeled them down to the very core, are fears of death. Fear of the unknown. As Mike Robinson, author of "The True Dynamics of Relationships" says:

"We need to understand losing our loved ones, reflects our deeper feelings of separation from the Divine. If you think about your loved ones, you will energetically connect with them. If you open your heart to receive, you may feel a presence or remember poignant moments shared, this is your loved ones responding. It is important not to get caught up in the new age spiritual belief that you mustn't grieve. You have lost a great friend so it is important to let out your feelings. Express and experience them and let them fly, for the phoenix always rises from the ashes"

This also applies to feelings of loneliness. Deep down it is separation from the Divine. These feelings are from your belief system, so use the Emotional Transformation Process to look within yourself. Take a look at the beliefs you have about separation from God/the Divine or the universe. We are all connected, it is the mind creating this illusion of separation. You have lost contact with your inner self, so start by getting to know and listening to the body. This is the path to freedom.

I have talked about reincarnation, don't just believe me, as this will become part of your belief system. You need to know it for yourself. When you know something you no longer fear it. We are all here for a purpose, here to evolve, and once you start listening inside you will have knowledge of the truth, instead of just believing it.

Many people who have had "near death experiences" have said they do not fear death any more. This is because they have faced it, and their consciousness becomes free. In the West we cover up death and older people don't like talking about it. When you suffer a loss of any kind, instead of putting on a brave face, accept how you feel, see the emotion behind it, you may feel angry, sad, an emptiness, but this feeling will gradually subside.

You have lived with yourself for how many years? But do you really know yourself?

Grieving, releases emotions and always release with love. Males, in particular, are often fearful of expressing emotions, especially if they listen to the old school glib advice saying *"pull yourself together, don't cry."*

Push those grey clouds up and away, allow the sun to shine!

Fear

As I have said before underlying all emotions is fear, fear of not being loved, fear of not being good enough, fear of not having enough, and fear of life in general.

Parents are frequently overtaken by fear for their children's health, well being and future. I have been in that situation myself. I was in my early thirties and constantly worrying. The "what if" thoughts were frequently about my children until self realisation stepped in, and my intuitive voice told me to stop. I was not living, I was just existing.

"To live is the rarest thing in the world. Most people exist, that is all"

Oscar Wilde

I found several books helpful at this time, including, "You Can Heal Your Life" by Louise Hay. My other recommendations are listed at the back of this book.

When faced with fear, try challenging it by not acting upon it. Instead go into the feeling of fear, breathe, and observe it. You are not the fear, it is only the mind creating it, so breathe into it until it subsides. If you react instead of accepting the fear and just being with it, it will take you over. Learning to focus inward on this feeling is difficult, but a shift will take place with practise and fear will gradually lose its power.

Fear is fear of loss, losing something, ultimately the fear of death, *being less.*

Robert Tennyson Stevens is the developer of a unique curriculum of empowerment techniques, designed to support you in manifesting, sustaining and enjoying life. He is author of "Conscious Language" and says any emotion fully felt will turn into its opposing strength. Grief turns into joy, fear turns into confidence and pain turns into love. When we stop resisting pain and surrender, a flow of energy within the body allows change to take place.

We have to master staying in the centre of the feeling we have as an observer, detached and accepting. We cannot stop fear or pain in our lives but we can be in charge of them, and not let them be in charge of us. It is acceptance of them without resistance, and when this happens we do not deplete our energy. When we resist and become caught up in the feelings, we use up a lot of energy in the experience of fear.

Spend a few minutes a day writing in your journal what you feel, or say it aloud to yourself. Fear hides in the body so expressing the fear is the first step to removing it. Angry, jealous, depressed, lonely people are filled with fear.

This is a good exercise to do several times a day:

Simple Mindfulness Exercise

- Sit in a comfortable position, close your eyes and scan your body. How does it feel? Any aches, pains or tension?

- How does your body feel emotionally. Happy, sad, lonely? Just go into the body and observe, don't judge

- Finally how is your mind? Quiet, busy, positive, negative?

- Take three deep breaths and open your eyes. Look at the colours around you. Listen. What do you hear? Feel if there are any anxieties within the body and just accept whatever you feel

- Try not to analyse but just be there in the moment. This is how we find self knowledge.

Regularly scanning the body throughout the day through this exercise will help you to gradually know your body, therefore releasing stress and anxieties more quickly.

We have all found ourselves in a situation of jealousy, whether it is a friend's new car, new house, or another friendship. Just be aware in the moment how you feel, and accept that is how you feel without judging yourself. Don't try and change anything, just keep breathing. Awareness of your feelings will bring change and transformation.

If you didn't have all your fears how different would your life be? You can start changing your life now by becoming aware in every moment, and paying attention to what's happening in your body!

We all rely on our mind to plan and organise and allow us to carry out our everyday tasks but contemporary society has allowed the mind to take over and cause unnecessary suffering.

If you are constantly fearful you will attract more of the same. The children that tend to have the most accidents are the ones with mothers that worry they will hurt themselves. Fear is energy and whoever you are fearful for will be surrounded by that negative energy, and attract even more. We bring our children into this world and act as their guardians but then they must be allowed to fly! Whatever they do or wherever they go is their soul's journey.

Instant communication and round the clock media activity brings the fear of natural and man made disasters around the planet right into our homes. The best we can possibly do for ourselves is to guard against being caught up in the media hype, as this affects our energy.

We can have empathy and compassion for those affected but not get drawn into fear of the situation, as this will only add to the confusion and slows down the healing process of everything and everyone concerned. Love, prayer and healing can be sent and I will explain this in more detail in Chapter 12 on Healing.

FREE YOURSELF FROM FEAR

1. Sit quietly where you will not be disturbed whilst doing this practice.

2. Take in three deep breaths and relax.

3. What are you most fearful of? Really feel the emotions and feelings of this fear, and on a scale of one to ten (one being not fearful and ten being terrified), how do you rate

this fear? This will allow you at the end to measure how much you have reduced it by.

4. Using both hands tap gently on both collarbones, whilst you are focusing on this fear, observing the feelings, don't worry about the situation just focus on the way you are feeling. Keep breathing deeply into it, watching the emotion as an observer. You are not this feeling, it is just energy that you have carried around for years. Do this for as long as the feeling is intense, it may be a few minutes or a little longer.

5. Once the feeling starts to subside continue tapping on the collar bones, look straight ahead keeping your head still, close and open your eyes.

6. Continue tapping keeping your head still, look with your eyes down to the left, then down to the right, move the eyes in a full circular clockwise movement and then anticlockwise, breathing deeply, still feeling any fear that you may still have.

7. Now hum the first two lines of the tune of "Happy Birthday". Count from one to five. This balances the right and left side of the brain. Take in a deep breath and let go.

8. Check on a scale of one to ten how you are now feeling.

9. Hopefully the scale will have reduced, but if not repeat this sequence until it is has dropped.

10. The intention is to release this feeling of fear you have been holding onto within your energy system, and is a tool for those who want to physically do something to help their situation. With practice in the future you can just go into any feeling and emotion, and change the energy by focusing and breathing into it.

Love

Pure, unconditional love is the only true emotion. Not superficial and possessive, pure unconditional love does not request anything in return. It is giving from the heart. The more you give out, the more you receive.

Love is our true essence. Watching a mother with her new born baby is an example of pure, unconditional love. It is uncritical, non judgemental and has no expectations. Some of the great masters such as Jesus, Gandhi and Mother Theresa had the ability to smile, speak kindly or gently touch someone and it would create healing. They had open hearts, so love would flow out and change those around them. This is how a healer works. If we learn to open our hearts it raises our consciousness and heals everything around us. Love is a state of being.

Exercise to Open the Heart

1. Sit quietly and take three deep breaths.

2. Place the palms of each hand, one on top of the other over the heart centre (middle of chest). This helps you to relax and releases the hormone oxytocin (hormone of love and peace).

3. Breathe in and out of the heart centre for two to three minutes. Every inhale, breathe in love, and exhale, send out love (say quietly to yourself, " love" on the in breath, "love" on the out breath). Simply visualise and really feel whatever makes your heart sing. This may be a new born baby, a flower, a holiday destination or a walk in the countryside. Bring this wonderful, alive feeling into the heart. Visualise the heart centre (between the breastbone) opening out like a flower when the sun shines.

4. Sit quietly and see if you feel more relaxed, lighter and expanded.

5. If you can do this three or four times a day over the next few weeks your heart centre will start to be more open.

I have felt and dowsed the energy of a person when they are thinking peaceful positive thoughts. Their heart centre opens and their aura can expand up to several metres. Yet when dwelling on negative thoughts, the aura may only be a few inches from the body. Even when feeling depressed, think of something that is good and brings you inner peace. This will become your reality.

Negative emotions such as anger and anxiety are counter productive to our immune system, whereas laughter and feelings of love can raise the antibodies, therefore helping the body to fight against infection. When we laugh, natural killer cells that destroy tumours and viruses increase. Love and laughter also increase serotonin and endorphin levels.

It is time now to move into a heart centred consciousness for better health. Unconditional love flows through your heart when you rise above daily consciousness and nothing physical affects this. There is only one kind of love which makes us feel whole. This is unconditional love, caring about someone, without any expectations or favours in return, it is given from the heart. When we genuinely give from the heart it raises our consciousness.

Each person that lives a heart centred life will raise the consciousness of thousands of people. Imagine the impact if several people in a neighbourhood or all the people in a town did this.

Self Love

This is what many of us are working on in this lifetime. Unless we love ourselves, we cannot love another. This is not about the ego and believing we are better than others in some way. It is forgiving yourself and accepting yourself for who you are, whatever physical appearance you have. We spend much of our time making judgements about ourselves and others, based on physical appearance.

Gratitude

Once you establish gratitude with a genuine feeling, it will raise your energy. It is useful to either keep a gratitude journal or add to your daily journal everything you are grateful for in your life. Every morning when I wake up and look out of my window I am genuinely grateful deep inside for my home, friends around me, family and the gift of life itself. In the depths of despair it is difficult to be grateful, but try to accept what has happened and let go.

If you find daily writing too much, try weekly, or a timetable to suit yourself. Gratitude is an expression of love. If when giving thanks to anyone say to yourself *"With Infinite Love and Gratitude I thank you for........"*. This is an immensely powerful way to open your heart, and love will flow through you. It is not just about being grateful for having more money or what you perceive as a better house than your friend. That's superficial and egotistical. I am talking about a deep sense of appreciation from your heart.

It is appreciating "in your life," which is in the moment.
Gratitude Transforms Your Being!

Your true spiritual essence resides in the vibration of love and gratitude, so continually be grateful for all you have and it will lift your spirit.

One morning on waking, try to imagine you know nothing and say to yourself, "I know nothing," therefore no belief system, no likes or dislikes and see everything with new eyes. See how it feels.

Enlightenment

Eckhart Tolle from his book, "The Power of Now" explains enlightenment simply in the following parable:

"A beggar had been sitting by the side of the road for over thirty years. One day a stranger walked by. "Spare some change?" mumbled the beggar,

mechanically holding out his baseball cap. "I have nothing to give you", said the stranger. Then he asked "What's that you are sitting on?", "Nothing", replied the beggar. "Just an old box I have been sitting on for as long as I can remember". "Ever looked inside" said the stranger. "No" said the beggar. "What's the point? There's nothing in there". "Have a look inside", insisted the stranger. The beggar managed to pry open the lid. With astonishment, disbelief, and elation, he saw that the box was filled with gold.

I am that stranger who has nothing to give you and is telling you to look inside. Not inside any box, as in the parable, but somewhere even closer: inside yourself.

"But I am not a beggar", I can hear you say.

Those who have not found their true wealth, which is the radiant joy of Being and the deep, unshakable peace that comes with it, are beggars, even if they have great material wealth. They are looking outside for scraps of pleasure or fulfilment, for validation, security or love, while they have a treasure within that not only includes all those things, but is infinitely greater than anything the world can offer. The word enlightenment conjures up some superhuman accomplishment, and the ego likes to keep it that way, but it simply is your natural state of felt oneness with Being. A state of connectedness."

The Buddha's simple definition of enlightenment is *"the end of suffering."* It is your deepest self, your true nature. You can know it when the mind is still, when you are in the present moment.

Observing daily our thoughts and emotions, both equally as important, with focused attention within is *"the doorway to being."*

Chapter 5

Living In The Present Moment

The past has gone and cannot be changed and we don't know what the future holds. We only have this moment. This is possibly the most difficult concept to grasp, as we all live by time. If there were no people on the planet but only trees and birds, the time would be now! Man has created time.

Worry only exists in the past or future. We tend to say if only I had done this or that, or worry about what may happen. Just simply being aware that you are thinking about the past or future will bring you back into the present moment. Deepak Chopra MD explains:

"The present moment transcends time. Every moment unfolds into the present moment, it never changes. What changes is the situation around the moment. If you separate the situation from the moment, then you have a corridor, a transformational vortex, this being the source to infinite creativity and joy."

Practise at least once a day for a week, a mindful exercise. If you are peeling the potatoes, brushing your teeth, or gardening, focus completely on what you are doing and keep the mind out of the way,. If you are gardening, look at the flowers, the weeds you pull out. Just be aware in your body and keep the mind still. How does this make you feel? If you have a busy mind just simply ask it to be quiet! Imagine the incessant chattering mind as a small yappy dog that is never silent. Every now and then just shout at it to be quiet. Again, write down in your journal how you get on. This should all help to expand your consciousness.

The constant chatter of the mind stops us from finding the stillness within. The mind creates the illusion of separateness. Undoubtedly the mind is a finely tuned instrument but can be destructive to the individual if used negatively. We have come to think we are our mind, and we most certainly are not. When we start watching the thinker our state of consciousness rises. Eckhart Tolle, author of "The 'New Earth" says:

"The key is to be in a permanent state of connectedness with your inner body-to feel it at all times. This will rapidly deepen and transform your life. The more consciousness you direct into the inner body, the higher its vibrational frequency becomes, much like a light that grows brighter as you turn up the dimmer switch, and so increase the flow of electricity. At this higher energy level, negativity cannot affect you anymore, and you tend to attract new circumstances that reflect this higher frequency.

If you keep your attention in the body as much as possible, you will be anchored in the Now. You won't lose yourself in the external world, and you won't lose yourself in your mind. Thoughts and emotions, fears and desires may still be there to some extent, but they won't take you over."

Try to step out of the time dimension as much as possible. Simply focus on your breathing or whatever you are doing in the moment. The more you do this the more you will find that stillness within, and start to detach from the turmoil going on in your life and the world.

We are all desperately searching for peace, yet generally nothing we do allows us to find peace. This is because it is not *doing* it is a state of *being* and the deeper inner feeling that is important.

Scientists have discovered a tribe of people in Brazil that have no concept of time in their culture. They were first contacted in 1986 and Professor Chris Sinha of the University of Portsmouth led the research. His article appeared in the journal "Language and Cognition." His findings centre on the Amondawa who have no words in their language to express our notions of "time," "weeks," "months" or "years." He says:

"We can now say without doubt that there is at least one language and culture which has no concept of time as we know it. They live in a world of events, rather than seeing events as being embedded in time. We have so many metaphors for time and its passing and say "the weekend is nearly gone", "she's coming up to her exams", "I haven't got the time", and so on. We have created these metaphors and they have become the way we think. The Amondawa don't talk or think like this. For these fortunate people time isn't money, they aren't racing against the clock, and they don't even discuss next week or next year. You could say they enjoy a certain freedom."

Maybe we could all learn from them!

You are not your mind

From time to time we may encounter people who appear to talk to themselves and we take this as symptom of mental disturbance or illness. Many more of us have this same conversation with ourselves but we don't say it out loud. This is the voice that belongs to your conditioned mind and all your past history and beliefs. It does not have any relevance on your life today, and is certainly taking you away from the present moment. This inner voice can keep you in the past, drain your energy and eventually lower your immune system.

We can free ourselves instantly by listening to that inner voice, looking out for the repetitive thought patterns that seem like a taped recording, playing over and over again. When we become aware of the same thoughts coming up again and again, it is a revelation. Who is watching those thoughts? We now move into a higher state of consciousness, the power of the thoughts diminishes, as we are not energising the mind.

With practise you will regain your birthright which is to have inner peace and calm.

We need the mind to carry out certain tasks, but once the task has been completed, come back into the present.

Mindfulness and Listening

Being mindful of everything you say and do is the key to unlocking your potential. It is not judging, thinking or reflecting. It is observing each moment and treating each moment like a new breath. With each breath there is a new present moment. The last breath is the last moment, gone forever, and cannot be changed, and the next breath is the future, which hasn't yet arrived.

One of the best ways to stay in the present moment is to consciously listen to everyone who speaks to us. Most of the time we tend not to do this. We may get the gist of the conversation, and then the mind tends to wander, especially if the speaker is not engaging us.

Truly listening to someone means allowing them to tell their story, without interruption and when they have finished you can participate. Are you one of these people who listens, then after a few minutes interrupts with your story or to make your point? Your friend may be telling you about a holiday in Paris, then whoosh, off you go, interrupting with the last time you went to Paris and how it rained and so on. The present moment is lost again. Most people simply do not know how to listen, because their attention is taken up by thinking. I know because I am one of those people and still have to be aware of listening with my inner self. Don't judge yourself if this happens, just accept it, then move on.

Relationships cannot survive and thrive if judgement and reproach come in, as the mind has taken over your life. Try the following exercise:

- ✦ When having a conversation with someone, breathe in and out deeply and calmly, listening to their every word

- ✦ Don't interrupt the conversation until they have come to the end of their story. We often do this if we feel an awkward silence

- Then respond if you wish in a calm manner. Your answer will then be more articulate, controlled and focused

- This is living in the moment with awareness.

Creativity

Children are naturally creative and express themselves in a spontaneous way. To be yourself is to be creative but gradually, as we grow older, the conditioning sets in. First you're told at school you can't sing so you are excluded from the choir. You are not good enough at football, so even your friends don't pick you for the team. Suddenly lack of self worth becomes part of your belief system.

There is beauty in the natural voice just as there is beauty in the trees and flowers. We live in a society of rules. Play music and allow yourself to move with it as you wish, see how it feels. You don't have to move in a particular sequence, just go with the flow. Try cooking without a recipe book, listen to your inner self, and add what you feel like. Go with the intuition, not the mind, and you will find you are a more creative cook than you realised. Stop worrying about what people may think.

Speaking Your Truth in the Moment

Speaking our truth is possibly one of the hardest things for humans to do, as we like to please. This is not about shouting and being rude to people but it is about saying how you really feel about a situation.

We can start speaking our truth immediately. When confronted by someone whose opinion differs try replying in a calm and positive manner along these lines:

"Yes I can see what you are saying, but personally I would prefer to do it my way" or, *"I would love you to visit my home sometime but I cannot do it*

this weekend' or,"I have decided to go away for Christmas this year. I know you have come to my house for ten years but I feel like a break myself."

If we don't listen to what our heart says, then we are not following our soul's pathway. The next time you receive an invitation that you would rather decline, pay attention to that inner voice.

We are often afraid of upsetting people, at the expense of upsetting ourselves. If they are offended it is not your issue. If you continue to people please, you dis-empower yourself. Listen to that inner body and be true to yourself. I have found over the years when people suppress speaking their truth, and are afraid to do so in case they are judged, it can often manifest in the physical body as a sore throat, a weak voice and more serious conditions if not dealt with.

Say what you feel, let go and don't feel guilty. Once we start speaking our truth in the moment we regain our freedom.

Chapter 6

Be A Creator Not A Victim

Be yourself as everyone else is taken
Oscar Wilde

Be Aware Of Your Body

The majority of people do not know their body. They may have spent seventy or eighty years nurturing their external body, but never given a thought to the inside. Once we become aware of our body we learn to tune into what messages it is giving us and act on them. We start creating a mind, body and spirit link, realising the connection brings harmony and peace within the body. Once we stop paying attention to these signals we fall into the trap of eating the wrong food, staying up too late, and abusing our bodies.

Take time to appreciate what our body does, and be truly grateful, as gratitude opens the heart. Go into your heart for emotional intelligence, not the head. If I am repeating myself several times in this book, it is because it has taken me twenty years or so to *really hear* and act on what I have learnt. Do the body awareness meditation daily as discussed in Chapter 3. Regularly ask yourself, "How does my body feel inside now?" If there is dis-ease inside, deal with it. The key to changing your life is having a permanent connectedness with the inner body. Once we direct our consciousness into the inner body, the more we raise our vibration.

Recreate and Rewrite Your Lifescript

When working with clients I demonstrate how to change a situation and not become a victim. Many of us remain in a place because we feel safe and fear prevents us from moving on and out of our comfort zone. If you are continually thinking of yourself as a vulnerable person who can't stand up for themselves, then you will create this as your reality.

The thoughts running through our minds daily about ourselves, become our life's intention. If we start to think of our partner as uncaring, or our child as being bad at sports, we are writing their lifescript for them. Psychologist William Braud, examined this question by gathering volunteers and asked them to carry out biofeedback on themselves, then with a partner. He found the mind over matter effect of thoughts had the same physical effect whether used on themselves or their partner.

Therefore our thoughts about others affect them also. This is why I mentioned earlier in the book, that having negative thoughts about family members can have a drastic impact and bring about the circumstances most feared. So change your "script" about yourself and others.

Start today by writing in a journal:

- How is your present life script affecting you and others around you? Are you happy, sad, peaceful or angry? What are your fears? What do you keep saying to yourself and others? Are you afraid of losing a friend or partner because of fear of being alone? Watch the thought patterns and write down everything you feel victimised for ie relationships, economy, health, lack of time. How can you change it?

+ Do the Emotional Transformation Process surrounding these emotions. Take charge and make a conscious decision

+ De-clutter your life, and if you find it difficult to let go, set yourself goals

+ What judgements do you have about yourself and your family? Are they valid?

+ Now rewrite a new script for yourself. Co-create your new reality. Do this with *intention*. The power of intention is empowering, making you feel you really can create your new reality. Write down in your journal your intention and how you are going to manifest your new life script

+ If it helps, ask the universe to assist with your new reality. Ask and you will receive! Be realistic and do not act from the ego

+ Also visualise your children and partner doing well at school and work, having friends and fun, and performing to the best of their ability

+ Set your intention of what you want in life with clarity and precision, and most importantly, act and feel as if this has happened. If you want peace within the family environment, visualise and feel the immense harmony around you, as well as feeling this within your own being

+ If you pray, instead of saying, "please will you bring me peace," as this is inferring sometime in the future, so will never manifest. Instead, give thanks and gratitude for the peace and harmony in your home now, as if it has happened. Start with yourself, bringing a sense of balance to your being, then it will affect all those around you

- I know I am repeating myself, but I want this to sink in. Don't change others, change yourself, then, others will change. They will not know why, but they will. If your partner, for example, is an angry person, look at yourself and where the anger is within you. Once you start releasing this and bringing more love into your life, it will have a knock on effect on everyone around you. So watch your own thoughts, judgements and actions. Try it and see

- Deal with your suppressed emotions, keep writing in your journal. When we release our own fears, everyone around us cooperates and is in harmony

- Keep your journal and see the changes in yourself and those around you.

Stop being a victim

Start by writing out everything you feel is wrong in your life. It could be tensions around your family, relationships, your health, the economy or your work and lack of leisure time. You can start today by simply making the decision not to be a victim. You are in charge of your life, no one else is to blame.

If you feel you are working twelve hours a day, seven days a week, then why? If it is something you love, then fine, if not, change the job. Little by little, start looking at areas in your life you are not at peace with and take action to change them. Just sitting and being depressed about your lot changes nothing.

Start listening to your heart and to what makes your heart sing, what you enjoy doing, who you like being with and what type of career you would like? Fear of the unknown can keep us in the same place, but sometimes we have to move out of our comfort zone and trust we will be looked after, which we will. Try to accept life as it unfolds to you.

Stop being angry and surrender to life. When we stop fighting and go with the flow of life, instead of feeling victimised, life takes on a different perspective.

If you are really struggling, ask the universe for help! If we are just *being* we are aware of our feelings in the moment. When my buttons are pressed, I imagine taking a step back out of my body, to observe the negative feeling in a detached way, see that it is only energy, this is not me, so I don't react, just allow the feeling to *be*, and breathe deeply letting go. Being aware dissolves the energy, and takes you to a new higher state of consciousness. Reacting and getting caught up in the turmoil will bring you to a lower level of consciousness. Don't beat yourself up if you do react, just try again next time.

One shift in consciousness I had was many years ago when I realised I had previously agreed on some level to incarnate into the life I have, choosing my parents and friends to learn my life's lessons and allowing my soul to evolve. Unfortunately when a soul incarnates, the memory of this is erased, otherwise life would be too simple with no purpose, and most importantly the soul would not evolve. It is knowing and understanding whatever happens is perfect and accepting this. Although this may be hard at times, acceptance allows us to live a more fulfilled life.

Ego

If you get an impulse to do something, this is the "higher mind" or intuition, so act upon it. It is usually the first thought that comes in when asking a question. Often the ego or "lower mind" will come in to contradict and knock you off course. I did have a very busy mind, with the ego trying to take over, until I decided to liken it to a yappy French poodle who demands attention. If you recognise this as you, give the dog a name then when you feel it taking over your life, just shout at it to be quiet because you are the master. When decisions have to be made always listen to your heart, don't follow the head. We all make mistakes in life but the ego doesn't like admitting them.

There are no mistakes in life, just detours! When we live by the ego, we cannot be completely stress free. Eckhart Tolle says:

"The most common ego identifications have to do with possessions, the work you do, social status and recognition, knowledge and education, physical appearance, special abilities, relationships, belief systems, political and other collective identifications. None of these are you. People strive after money, possessions, power, to feel better about themselves. Even when they attain these things, they find the hole is still there, that it is bottomless"

Continually listen to the heart, then, you are following your soul's pathway and going with the flow of life. You can try a simple exercise to develop your ability to listen to your intuitive voice. The next car journey you take, ask yourself which route shall I take today? Several years ago when I did this, I went to the end of my road and asked inwardly, *which way shall I go to work?* My intuitive voice said, turn left, (when I usually go right). Immediately my head came in and said, *no go right you always do, and it's the quickest route,* so off I went, ignoring the inner voice, and half a mile away the road was blocked by an accident, and I was stuck in traffic. From then on I listened!

We come into this world with nothing but love. We leave this world with nothing but love. In between the ego keeps us trapped, it likes to control like narcissism. Get out of the ego now and set yourself free!

Detachment

This is not about being cold, indifferent or not caring about anything. It is an inner state of calmness and observing what is going on without judgement, therefore not getting caught up in any emotional scenarios. This can be very hard with personal relationships, as we are all human.

How many hours or days have we spent becoming angry and frustrated, worrying about useless thoughts and feelings due to lack of detachment? A beneficial way of practising is in the simple meditation given earlier, where you sit quietly, and watch your thoughts as an observer. You are not getting involved, just watching and allowing your thoughts to pass by like the flow of a river and they will start to lose their power over you.

Letting Go

I would like to quote from Wayne W. Dyer Ph.D author of "The Power of Intention" on the subject of letting go:

"Perhaps the greatest lessons of my life have revolved around the slogan of the recovery movement: "Let Go and Let God"-a notion that involves relinquishing ego's attachment to, or fear of, something. The single most pronounced attachment for most of us during the morning of our lives is the attachment to being right! There's nothing the ego loves more than to be right, which makes it an important and satisfying attachment to practise letting go of."

The ego thinks being right is being happy, but in fact, the opposite is true.

If we all gave up desiring to be right, we would create world peace. Desire is the cause of all suffering. You could try an exercise next time you find yourself in a disagreement with a friend or family member. Write in a journal the nature of the argument, then:

- a. write the disagreement from your perspective
- b. write from the other persons perspective
- c. from an independent observer

In order to give up being right, do you feel you are gaining or losing something? It may help to sit quietly or meditate upon how you feel in the body. Where do you hold onto tensions?

Attachments are habits and restrict your spiritual development. So many of us desire a big house, smart car, expensive clothes and possessions, which is fine, but attachment to these things can be destructive. In having an expensive sports car do you genuinely appreciate the quality and work that has gone into its manufacture, or do you simply like the status that it gives you amongst your peers? If the latter, this is attachment.

An attachment is about your own needs, fears and insecurities. Some parents are so attached to their children, as we discussed earlier, they never leave them to explore life. Therefore children are prevented from becoming independent and establishing their own identities.

Observation without judgement

This has been referred to several times in this book, so I would like to explain what is meant by it. If we didn't have any belief system we would look at people and only see the beauty within, the truth of them, their soul.

We may not like the personality or behaviour of individuals but they all still have a divine essence. You do not have to choose them as your close friends, but we can accept who they are, without judgement. Try to see the good in everyone. They are on their pathway as you are on yours and no one is any better or worse than anyone else.

If they affect you, or press your buttons, then deal with it. We must accept every person and situation as an opportunity to grow spiritually.

The modern media can cause negative self analysis as they encourage us to worship celebrities and criticise ourselves. We can be discerning and use the good judgement we all have to recognise this manipulation.

We tend to mirror people and they us. Try this simple exercise:

Think of someone you know who annoys you, or some one you feel envious of. Sit quietly and whilst thinking of them without any judgement, start to see how you are feeling, where and what emotions are coming up. Then follow the Emotional Transformation Process to help you to deal with whatever is going on in your own energy system.

If we are self conscious when we are in front of other people, it is because we have a fear of being judged. Often we are the ones doing the judging. Start looking at yourself and be aware when you start to criticise others. Once you become aware of this, something changes. Judgements are beliefs created with the mind which can escalate out of control, without self awareness.

We often criticise to make ourselves feel better, so look at the root cause of this in yourself. Is this how you show your fear of not being good enough? This can stem from self judgement. Do you beat yourself up when you haven't lived up to your own high expectations?

Start speaking in the moment or writing out how you feel. Get it out and be conscious the next time you judge. Accept you may have done so, but don't allow inner tension to build up or punish yourself. If we look at a person in the street without any judgement, we are sending out love. Observation is love. If we could all do this, we would certainly heal the world.

Envy and Jealousy

We all have feelings of envy and jealousy throughout our lives. As children we have been conditioned to be competitive, so a belief system has been created. Maybe a comparison was made as to how good you were at school, academically, or at sport? Possibly you were judged or self judged, therefore you were made to feel not good enough, or a failure, which has left feelings of insecurity or envy at what others have achieved. There is no such thing as failure. Stop the mind controlling you.

It can be very difficult to let go of past jealousies and it can cause much upset with the mind controlling you, allowing the old record to go round and round. To set yourself free, just observe the situation which makes you feel envy, accept it completely, without judgement. The feeling will start to change energetically, so you can start to let go. If we still hold onto an opinion about something, the mind will keep bringing up the past situation, or someone will keep pressing your buttons, until you do something about it, so act now and deal with it. When it no longer upsets you, you have dealt with it.

Forgiveness

We achieve inner health only through forgiveness-the
forgiveness not only of others but also of ourselves.
Joshua Loth Liebman

Past hurts and the blame we attach to parents, friends, colleagues and partners can literally eat away at us and affect our health if we hold onto these negative feelings.

Why let the suffering continue. Can you forgive? It is important to accept what has happened. It has passed and without suppressing the feelings you have, try to let go of the connection which caused the pain. When you hold onto resentment of someone, you are bound to them energetically, so wherever our thoughts of anger are, our energy goes.

Stop and regain your energy before you hurt yourself by not letting go.

See people through the eyes of your soul to another soul, their true essence is pure but you do not have to like their personality as I have said before, so move on, empower yourself, and regain the freedom to grow.

The Emotional Transformation Process will help with the feelings you have around this situation. It may help as well to do 11 x 22s, as described in Chapter 3, which is clearing the patterns of the subconscious mind. Mike Robinson in "The True Dynamics of Relationships" says:

"To forgive can be painful, but not as painful as holding on to a judgement. To keep a polluted emotion held within the energy bodies makes us feel heavy, dirty, and sluggish. Look back over your life and ask who you need to forgive. Can you feel sadness, bitterness, anger and hurt? Write two letters to the person. The first letter include all your negative thoughts, emotions, swear words included, then a second letter which will include your words of forgiveness. Now burn the first one and let go of the energy you have held onto and decide whether to send the second one or burn it."

One of the hardest challenges we face is to forgive ourselves. It is through guilt we feel we have to punish ourselves. Accept what you did was right at the time. No judgement, just let go and love yourself as the beautiful being you are.

Forgiveness is to stop carrying the baggage of an experience or holding others responsible. These are your experiences. Forgive, and your energy lightens, and you start to see life through clear glass instead of dirty distorted mirrors. Use the Emotional Transformation Process to sit quietly and go into the feelings you have about forgiveness. Where can't you let go? How does it feel? Just observe the feeling and look behind the cause, at the truth.

Be Who You Are

From a course of study with Claire Montanaro, author of "Spiritual Awakening," I learned how to see myself for who I am, and be myself.

We are all busy and never have enough time, but between our appointments and commitments, find a period, preferably a day, but do what suits you, to ask your inner self the following:

+ Which job is the priority today? Listen to your intuition not the mind. Stop thinking which job has priority as you are using logic, instead go internally

+ Look in your wardrobe and feel which colours you want to wear and what makes you feel good

+ Eat when you feel hungry not when the clock tells you, and eat what you feel like. Ask is this the right food for me at this moment? Eat with awareness, chew your food slowly and enjoy it. By eating very slowly, chewing food consciously and enjoying it, may help you lose weight

+ Go to bed when you are tired

+ Try not to set an alarm to wake you, (unless an appointment or work)

+ Throughout the day ask yourself, what do I feel like doing today? And do it

+ Take note of everything around you, be aware

+ Whatever you do, do slowly, calmly, in an unhurried way, and breathe deeply every so often throughout the day

This is called going with the flow of life, and by listening to your inner voice will cause profound changes. Following your life's path means allowing everything to flow, and trusting that what needs to be done *will* still get done, but without the need to rush around, chasing your tail!

Acceptance

Following on from forgiveness is acceptance. Once you accept yourself for who you are you are able to accept others for who they are. As long as at all times you have tried to do your best for yourself and others, taking full responsibility, and accepting what happens in life is as it should be, this is liberating.

We all had experiences to go through in the past, but generally we did what we felt was right at the time. Maybe looking back you may have done things differently, but you were learning and that is why we are here on earth, to learn and evolve through the choices we make. So accept this, let go and move on.

Abundance

To bring more abundance into your life start acting and feeling as if you already have it. This is not about material wealth, although the same principles apply. Our thoughts create our inner world, and the way we talk and act creates our outer world. Everything you see around you will subconsciously impress upon you the idea of poverty or wealth. Keep signs of abundance in your environment.

When you bring the feeling of abundance in your being you will perpetuate the conditions of abundance in your reality, on the other hand if you are constantly feeling unworthy or a lack of it in your life, this will manifest. Your actions will also create subconscious impressions of abundance or lack of it, so choose them wisely, knowing you are worthy.

Developing self esteem

1. Choose an anchor, this is a physical action that you will use to "switch" on the feeling you want to have. Make it simple such as making a fist, rubbing your hands or pressing together your forefinger and thumb.

2. Sit quietly, relax and breathe deeply three times.

3. Select an event in the future where you want to feel better, perhaps more confident, enthusiastic, successful or motivated.

4. Select the feeling you want to have for this occasion.

5. Look back at a time when you felt that way, full of confidence.

6. Remember the experience clearly, notice the sounds, colours, textures and your feelings at the time. Hold onto the experience and really feel how you felt.

7. Allow this good feeling of confidence and self esteem to really fill the mind and body, allowing it to be as intense as possible, then, perform your anchor.

8. This links the physical action with the feelings.

9. Repeat 6 and 7 until a firm connection between the feeling and anchor are made. You may have to practise several times.

10. Whenever you want to recall this good feeling perform the anchor

Chapter 7

Create Optimum Health

"Our Body Has An Internal Pharmacy"
Dr Norman Shealy

You Are What You Eat

If you put the wrong fuel in a car it will never run to its optimum performance and indeed it may break down altogether. It is the same with the human body. Feed with the best fuel and everything will run smoothly. Optimum nutrition is giving your body the very best intake of nutrients to work efficiently. There are general guidelines for a balanced diet but we are all unique, all requiring different food intakes.

Life is about **balance** and this applies to our diet. As we become more aware, connecting and listening to our inner body, our overall health will start to improve. Next time you shop or choose food to eat, listen to the body and ask yourself, "which food is good for me right now?" Do this daily to ensure you eat what is good and nutritious for your body. We all have "binge" days but don't self criticise, just accept you are human and need a treat occasionally!

A balance in colours, textures and flavours are good guidelines. If the meal is the same colour you are most likely missing valuable nutrients. We need to be eating foods that sustain a healthy life force, as many ingredients bought nowadays have no energy within them. The reason being they are not as fresh as they could be and may have been on the supermarket shelves longer than is ideal. Check date stamps on produce and try to source locally.

Avoid genetically modified foods, and foods with preservatives. Ideally eat organic, and if not, then wash fruit and vegetables very well. You could start by growing a few of your own vegetables. A change in society has already begun and more and more of us are already doing this. If you don't have a garden, then try indoors with a few pots. The taste and nutrient content will be totally different to commercially grown vegetables and the food will be more alive with good energy.

Diets

We were not designed to wake up with an alarm clock, bolt down breakfast, grab a quick cup of coffee and then charge off to work. Life in general has become a slave to time but try, for at least a week, to eat when you feel hungry, instead of by the clock and eat what you feel your body requires.

One of the most important practices is to chew food slowly and thoroughly. Enjoy every mouthful and focus in the moment on what you are eating. This is Conscious Eating! Try to eat without watching television or reading, as you are not listening to when the body says you have eaten enough. You are not being conscious of the food you are eating. Just enjoy the flavours and different textures in your mouth. You can even lose weight doing this!

Obviously if you are socialising or eating with your family it is more difficult, but do your best. Occasionally we need to treat ourselves and the odd cream cake or chocolate bar is fine. Accept this, do not punish yourself or feel guilty afterwards.

If you are overweight, look at your thoughts or belief system. Do you often say, "Look at me I'm getting fat" or, "I only need to look at a cream cake and I put on weight," or refuse to look in a mirror. Stop punishing yourself or putting negative thought patterning into the subconscious mind. Instead listen to the inner dialogue with your body, of what it requires to be healthy, then the pounds will drop off. Some people pile on the weight due to underlying suppressed emotions. If this is so, look at what's behind the emotion and deal with it. Visualise yourself getting thinner, but more importantly feel it inside, really feel and act as if you are losing weight.

In many cases, excessive overeating or drinking can be emotional, so next time you reach for an extra bag of crisps, chocolate, or glass of wine, take a few seconds and breath three deep breaths to see how you are feeling. Why do you feel you need much more? Everything in moderation is absolutely fine, but be aware if there is an emotional response which is leading to excess.

If this is the case write down in your journal how you are feeling when this happens. What feelings are you trying to hide? Is it lack of self worth which makes you feel you have to be the comedian on a night out? We have all been there. Once in a while is fine, but don't make it a habit as this leads to inbalance in the body.

We have to honour the food we put into our body. Have gratitude for what you eat or drink. Respect the time it has taken for vegetables and fruit to be grown and animals to be reared. Whenever you cook, cook with love. Have you ever eaten a meal by someone who was in a bad mood and then served it up? The taste is completely different than one made by someone who cared for the ingredients and cooked with enjoyment, appreciation and love.

I always bless the food I cook, which actually changes its energy to a higher level. There is a reason some people say grace before they eat and whether they are aware of it or not, showing respect and gratitude for what is about to be eaten changes the life force of the food. So be observant and aware. Allow your choice of food and ingredients to be from your heart, your inner self, and not the mind or connected with emotions.

Ask yourself how your body feels. If you constantly feel sluggish and tired, look at your diet. If you are eating what your physical body requires, then you will be happier and have a lighter vibration which will add to your longevity! Always be grateful and give thanks to your physical body for all the support it provides for you in life. Do not just take it for granted.

I recommend a book called "The China Study" by Dr T. Colin Campbell, one of the most comprehensive studies of nutrition ever conducted, outlining startling implications for diet, weight loss and long term health.

Acid/Alkali Balance

One of the most important measurements of your health is the pH of your blood and tissues, which means how acidic or alkali it is. Rolf Gordon is the author of "CANCER-The Full Menu." This is a book recommended by Dr Patrick Kingsley, cancer specialist, who has dealt with around 3,000 cancer patients during thirty years of practice. Rolf says:

"The acid alkali of your blood must be dealt with to prevent you getting cancer or if you have cancer, most cancer patients have acidic blood, especially if they have had chemotherapy. The acid/alkali balance is measured on a pH (potential hydrogens) scale from 1 (very acidic) to 7.4 (neutral), to 10 (very alkaline). 7.4 to 7.5 are slightly alkaline and associated with good health. Cancer likes an acid environment."

High stress levels can produce an acidic environment in the body. This is another important reason for keeping a stress free life. Eating the wrong foods can also create too much acid within the body. As part of my work I dowse remotely to check a person's acid/alkali balance, and give suggestions on how to achieve the correct level. If pH tissue deviates too far to the acid side, oxygen levels decrease and body cells will start to die. A more alkaline body will allow oxygen to flourish. Cancer cannot survive in oxygen.

If the body is too acidic, it will cause minerals to be lost such as calcium, sodium, potassium and magnesium, causing some of the following problems:

+ Cardiovascular damage

+ Weight gain

+ Bladder and kidney infections

+ Immune deficiency

+ Hormonal problems

+ Premature ageing

+ Arthritis and other joint pain

+ ME

+ Low energy

+ Digestive problems

+ Candida and many more

Helicobacter pylori lives in an acid environment and is the main culprit in causing ulcers, and reducing Vitamin C in the system, so more reason to maintain an alkali body.

Hydrochloric acid can help digest food and help kill Helicobacter pylori as can ginger, apples, apple cider vinegar, good quality aloe vera, mastic gum, cabbage juice and broccoli sprouts. In a recent study published in the journal "Cancer Prevention Research," John Hopkins, Institute researcher Jed W. Fahey M.S ScD and a team of scientists, concluded that eating a daily dose of broccoli sprouts reduced the level of HpSA (a highly specific measure of the presence of Helicobacter pylori) by forty per cent.

Cabbage contains Vitamin U, (anti ulcer vitamin), and high amounts of glutamine which aids the healing of the gastro-intestinal tract. For a long time cabbage juice has been found to be beneficial for the treatment of constipation and ulcers. M. Verbach in his book, "Healing Through Nutrition," reported that cabbage was found to speed the healing of ulcers by ninety two per cent compared to thirty two per cent in non treated ulcer cases. Another product, Aloe Vera, aids the treatment of stomach/digestive disorders, and also helps wound healing, both internally and topically. Always use a good quality product as many on the market are diluted.

The human body is alkaline but all its functions produce acid, so we are constantly having to watch what we eat and drink. The perfect pH is 7.35 to 7.45, with a range of 1-14, one being the most acidic. You can obtain pH strips either from the internet, or at www. nutricentre.co.uk and they can also be purchased from many other outlets. To lower acidity keep alcohol, coffee, stress and negative emotions to a minimum. Refer to www.phmiracleliving.com for further information.

We should all eat more alkali foods, especially arthritis sufferers. If you have arthritis, take two tablespoons of organic apple cider vinegar in warm water to help maintain an alkali body. Most inflammation is caused by high acidity. If you follow a more alkali diet you generally sleep better, feel much more alert and are more focused.

Below are my tips on achieving and maintaining a healthy pH.

How to have a Healthy pH

- Try to eat daily seventy to eighty per cent alkali foods such as wholegrain products, quinoa and lentils, pearl barley, green and white tea, watermelons, almonds, seeds, fresh vegetables, fruit, green and herbal teas and other plant food. Remember Green is Good!

+ Oily fish is good and lean meat, such as chicken is only slightly acidic

+ Lemons and vinegar turn into alkali in the body. Squeeze the juice of half a lemon into a glass of warm water first thing in the morning to alkalise the body and help burn off fat. To give a boost to the immune system add half an inch of grated ginger and manuka honey, at least 15+Active. Manuka honey has a rating system called unique Manuka factor (UMF), to help distinguish between ordinary manuka honey and active manuka honey. UMF rating is the indicator to the strength of the antibacterial effect. A rating of 15+ or more is considered suitable for therapeutic medical use

+ Acidic foods are generally red meat, dairy, sugar, processed and refined foods, fizzy drinks, coffee, alcohol and eggs. Limit this intake to no more than twenty to thirty per cent per day

+ Alkaline juices made from green vegetables/grasses

+ Living in a house with Geopathic Stress (discussed in a later chapter), can cause acidic blood

+ Bicarbonate of soda (without aluminium) is excellent to alkalise the body. For seven to ten days take one to two teaspoons in a small glass of water first thing in the morning, half an hour before food. If your pH is very low take two teaspoons first thing in the morning for seven days, then one teaspoon for a further seven days

+ Reduce stress levels, as this causes acidity in the body

+ Bicarbonate of soda is an excellent antidote to colds and flu. On the onset of flu take one to two teaspoons of bicarbonate of soda, in a glass of water, four times a day. On the second day repeat, on the third day three times a day, then twice a day, then half a teaspoon a day until better

+ According to Dr Tullia Simonini, the famous oncologist in Rome, who discovered the main cause of cancer to be fungus, based his treatment in 1983, on one of the strongest antifungal substances, bicarbonate of soda, which hits cancer cells with a shock wave of alkalinity, allowing more oxygen into the cells which cancer cells cannot tolerate

+ If the body is too acidic it will leach calcium and alkali from the bones

+ Calcium in milk and animal protein will leach calcium out of the bones, so if you have osteoporosis, opt for calcium from other sources such as green leafy vegetables, nuts and seeds. A cup of sesame seeds contains 2,200mg of calcium, compared to a cup of milk with around 280mg of calcium. For strong bones these are healthier options to obtain calcium

+ Do deep breathing, exercise and drink plenty of water to maintain good alkalinity.

Well Balanced Diet

Many years ago we could eat a very well balanced diet, as all the nutrients were abundant in the soil, and naturally transferred to our vegetables. Animals were also reared in natural environments.

Unfortunately today there are many processed, refined and adulterated foods on the market. The food industry adds high proportions of sugar, salt, colourings and many additives to their products and we have no control over this. Because our lives are so busy we spend less time preparing fresh food, so our health has been affected

According to Patrick Holford, the founder of The Institute for Optimum Nutrition in Richmond, Surrey:

"In the UK alone over £400 million a year is spent on pesticides, which is quite frightening. Pesticide exposure is associated with depression, memory decline, destabilisation of moods and aggressive outbursts, Parkinsons disease, and in addition according to Professor William Rea, thoracic and cardiovascular surgeon, (with a strong passion for the environmental aspects of health disease), so is asthma, eczema, irritable bowel syndrome and rhinitis. Forty percent of pesticides, it now has been proven are cancer promoting"

Organic food is the answer, but if you don't buy organic it is sensible to wash all fruit and vegetables extremely well.

Over thirty or forty years ago we got all the selenium required to protect the heart, directly from our diet. Nowadays most of this mineral is depleted because the land on which food is grown has been subjected to harmful chemicals and pesticides. We can obtain enough selenium by eating about five brazil nuts per day.

The long term debate on genetically modified foods is ongoing, but my personal view is that GM is not the way forward, and I would advise against these products.

General Health Tips

- Avoid aluminium contained in many deodorants as this may have a link with breast cancer. Check they do not contain propyl alcohol. Shaving can increase the absorption of these products. I recommend using a natural deodorant and there are some on the market that use the properties of pure alum mineral salts

- Look at Thermography as an alternative to Mammograms, as it doesn't use radiation

- Be discerning with medical drugs. The pharmaceutical industry is an extremely profitable business, and it does not always put health concerns above making money

- Ideally do not use microwaves for cooking, and don't warm babies' bottles in one! It changes the chemical structure of foods as well as causing a loss of nutrients

- Aloe Vera can be used in a variety of ways. Externally for wounds, cuts, and bites and even cutting the leaf of a fresh plant and rubbing the gel onto the affected part of the body. Taken internally, it is an immune booster or useful for aiding digestive problems. Ensure the Aloe Vera you purchase is labelled at the top of the list of ingredients, and is certified by the International Aloe Science Council

- If you take vitamins and minerals take a good quality food form, as opposed to synthetic. A liquid supplement or powder to mix with water is better

- Don't take sugar in your diet and read food labels as sugar is often hidden in fruit juices, cereals, tomato sauce and other products. Sugar is an "inverted fertiliser" for certain bacteria so limit fructose consumption to below twenty five grams a day if in good health, and below fifteen grams if you have high blood pressure, heart disease or other ill health

- Useful websites for more health information are, Dr Norm Shealy www.normshealy.com and Dr Joseph Mercola, www.mercola.com

- For good quality vitamins and minerals I would recommend contacting Nutricentre, Higher Nature, Biocare or Lamberts. They have nutritionists who can advise free of charge

+ Manuka honey, at least Active 15+, (higher levels can destroy MRSA), has excellent antibacterial/antibiotic properties, boosts the immune system, and can be used externally for fungal infections and ulcers

+ Avoid eating burnt, and fried foods as much as possible. The odd barbecued burger is fine, but burning food not only loses vital nutrients, but may lead to increased levels of carcinogens that can cause cancer

+ If you suffer from digestive problems such as IBS or diverticulitis, try to avoid bran based cereals as they are too harsh on the digestive system. Try oat cereals such as porridge, with no added sugar

+ Turmeric is an excellent antioxidant and contains the anti-inflammatory compound curcumin

+ Avoid transfats and hydrogenated oils (found in some margarines and processed foods). Read the food labels

+ Oxytech from Dulwich Health is good for candida, bloated stomachs and IBS or Oxy-Powder from www.thenha.com

+ After a course of antibiotics take a good probiotic (from a reputable health store), which will replace the good bacteria destroyed by the antibiotics. Take for two to three months, and ensure an alkali diet

+ If taking statins for cholesterol, take CoQ10 at least 60-100mg, in the form of ubiquinol, not ubiquinone. Statins, which I do not particularly recommend for cholesterol, deplete the body of this nutrient, so ensure you take sufficient to help with any muscle wasting. The myth of cholesterol can be found on both Dr Joseph Mercola's and Dr John Briffa's website. CoQ10 also is significant in boosting the immune system

- Colloidal silver kills MRSA, and is a good antibacterial product

- Dr Marilyn Glenville is useful for womens' health problems www.marilynglenville.com

- The herb Pau d'Arco is excellent for healing candida

- With arthritis or osteoporosis it is best to keep to an alkali diet. Don't smoke as this makes the body acidic and try to keep stress to a minimum. Avoid cured meats, processed sugars and bleached flour

- A useful website is www.saveourbones.com where you can download the Natural Bone Building Handbook free! Avoid milk, as it leaches calcium out of the bones. Eat seeds, nuts, kale and other green vegetables. 2 tsp. chopped fresh basil will provide 60mg calcium. If inflammation is present, essential fatty acids will help.

- Most people are low in Omega 3 so ensure you take this, preferably in liquid form (usually higher in EPA/DHA, essential for good health). If it smells fishy the quality may be impaired so should not be taken.

Parasites

Dr Hulde Clark PhD wrote in her book, "The Cure of All Diseases," that she only found two things wrong when checking patients: **pollutants and pesticides.** She describes over ten years ago, discovering the true cause of cancer, being the fluke parasite. The parasite typically lives in the intestine, where it may be quite harmful, causing for example, colitis, crohns disease or irritable bowel syndrome, or may do no harm, but if it invades the liver, kidneys or uterus can do a great deal of harm.

Propyl alcohol is an antiseptic ingredient found in most cosmetic products such as shampoo, shaving lotions, deordorants, body creams, toothpaste, make-up and mouthwashes. The purpose is to inhibit microbial growths and extend shelf life. Practitioners are seeing beneficial results from removing the patient from these toxins in the home, and other chemicals causing environmental sensitivity. Flukes appear to multiply in people with propyl alcohol in their bodies. So start checking labels and steer clear of pollutants as much as possible. Avoid anything with "prop" at the beginning of it.

It would do no harm for most people especially with ill health to have a parasite cleanse. There are many available. Either contact the previous websites given, or check with a good health store. Dulwich Health sell a product called "AlliTech" which is 100% stabilised extract from garlic, excellent in killing all types of microbes, is antibacterial, antiviral, a good antibiotic, and helps build the immune system. Black walnut hull, usually sold as a tincture, is also a good parasite cleanse.

We all have a small percentage of parasites within our body, which is essential. When working with clients I check their levels through dowsing. Other methods are available such as vega testing, kinesiology (muscle testing) or a stool test. Most people who have cancer have a high proportion of micro parasites. Micro parasites will flourish if geopathic stress is present in a property, so eliminating this is of paramount importance and is discussed in a later chapter.

Drink lots of water to flush out toxins and wash hands regularly. Liquid soap containers are best, as parasites can live on bars of soap. Outdoor shoes should be left outside the house.

Skin Products

It is very important to watch your diet, but equally imperative to be careful what you put on your skin. Check label and avoid anything with parabens. Parabens are used in cosmetics to lengthen shelf life.

It is thought they can imitate the effects of oestrogen, so particularly significant for women.

Natural Face Lift

1. Breathe deeply three times and on each exhalation, with a sharp, short breath, open the mouth as wide as possible, sounding HAH.

2. Gently tap with both hands, using the fingertips in a circular motion, starting at the base of the neck, and working to the forehead. This stimulates the acupuncture points on the face.

3. Gently massage both ears with the fingertips, starting at the lobes, working at the back of the ears as well as the front and inside the ear. This will boost the immune system, give a feeling of well being and relax the whole body.

I recommend a useful website www.ewg.org/skindeep which is an excellent cosmetics database and good comparison of many products.

Conscious living slows down the ageing process. Consciousness pervades every cell when we live mindfully, allowing intelligence to flow through. The only thing that stops you accessing this intelligence, the infinite power you have is the ego. The ego likes to control and perpetuate the belief of separation, the past and future. It tells us when we reach a certain age to expect more wrinkles and aching bones, we then start mentally preparing and accepting this to be true. Don't fight it, just be, and live as much as possible consciously, in control of your life, feeling rejuvenated and in the moment. By doing this allows your spirit fully into the body, and the stress of life will cease.

Water

Water is a basic necessity for life. We can obtain a certain amount from food and fluids, but the majority of us need to increase our intake.

Tiredness, stiff joints, constipation and dry skin can suggest the underlying cause may be dehydration, so try increasing the consumption of water first to see if this helps. We require water to carry vital nutrients, oxygen and hormones to various parts of the body. A dry mouth is one of the last indicators of dehydration. Your organs will not function adequately without sufficient water. You are not only what you eat, but also what you drink!

There are varying reports on how much water our body is composed of and this can range from 63% to 80%. When we are born it is nearer to 75 to 80%, but depletes as we get older. Dr F. Batmanghelidj has spent years investigating the need for drinking plenty of water and his book, "Your Body's Many Cries for Water," is interesting reading. He says you are not sick, you are thirsty, as water keeps us healthy and pain free.

Deciding which water system is best is a bit of a minefield. Many people have the charcoal water filters which are fine to start with, but will not get rid of hormones, beta-blockers, antibiotics, birth control pills, and many other drugs.

There is much talk about the reverse osmosis system which can remove many substances. Elizabeth Brown, author of "Dowsing-The Ultimate Guide for the 21st Century," an excellent beginners' book, as well as for the more advanced dowser, has explored the world of water and recommends a purifying system from CIR, based near Plymouth. This uses imploded water technology, which removes contaminants and toxins. Here's a chance for budding dowsers to get out the dowsing rods and check which water is best for you!

Most uncooked vegetables and fruit contain about 90% water, but the climate you live in and time of year can also determine how much water you require. I suggest small amounts regularly throughout the day otherwise the kidneys will be overloaded! Rolf Gordon has this to say:

"Chlorine in water can injure red blood cells and damage their ability to carry vital oxygen to where it is needed. Putting in a tiny amount of Vitamin C powder can neutralise chlorine and will cut out its taste and odour. Chlorine also evaporates quickly in the open, so after leaving the glass of water for 20 minutes, it will have evaporated. Water from plastic bottles should be avoided as it can be contaminated with chemicals from the plastic, or the chemicals they clean the bottles with before use. According to Dr Hulde Clark, micro parasites feed on some of these chemicals. Water in glass bottles is fine: choose a natural mineral water that does not contain sweeteners".

Drink water at room temperature rather than ice cold as it is more easily accepted by the body. Take several sips throughout the day to maintain hydration rather than gulping pints of it down in one go.

Unless you are taking vitamin B2 (riboflavin), which turns urine bright yellow, it should remain light pale yellow. If it is a dark bright yellow you are not drinking enough water. If you haven't urinated fully or for several hours then drink more water.

As you get older check you are drinking plenty of pure water, not from sugary fruit juices. Sodas, coffee and tea contain caffeine, and will therefore act as a diuretic and dehydrate further.

Ozonated water is recommended in Rolf Gordon's book, "CANCER the full menu." It destroys the Norovirus, energises and hydrates. It is easily made with an ozonator and flushes toxins from the body very quickly. Available from Commercial Science www.comsci.org.uk.

A Becks Silver Zapper is also mentioned on the site. Dr Bob Beck claims this will purify the blood of all invaders such as bacteria, virus, HIV and parasites. It allows you to make your own colloidal silver, which has antiseptic and antimicrobial properties. This can be sprayed onto hands to protect against harmful bacteria and administered internally, to boost the immune system. It can also be used to cleanse toothbrushes by dipping into the solution.

Chapter 8

Immune System and Body Cleansing

The immune system does an excellent job of protecting the body against the micro organisms that cause disease.. To function at its optimum it requires balance and harmony. Healthy mucous membranes both in the digestive and respiratory tract are the first tissues to be attacked by micro organisms, so these areas must be strong.

The Lymphoid, part of the immune system, comprises a network of vessels that carry a clear fluid called Lymph, in one direction towards the heart. This network connects the spleen, tonsils, thymus gland and a multitude of lymph nodes, which generally appear in clusters around the neck, armpits and groin.

Boosting the immune system

+ Exercise- extreme vigorous exercising suppresses the immune system. According to Professor David Niemen, of Appalachian State University, moderate exercise can increase immunity, whereas intense exercise can reduce immunity, as the body produces certain hormones that temporarily lower the immune. Try gentle techniques such as yoga, Tai Chi or Qigong

+ Stress, depression and grief all suppress the immune system -eliminate as much stress as possible from your life. Try relaxation and meditation to relieve stress.

+ It is useful for women to take a good probiotic if taking the contraceptive pill or HRT. Also 15-25mg zinc, and

50mg Vitamin B6 or as advised by a natural health practitioner.

+ Diabetics taking medication for their condition should take 50-200mg CoQ10, Vitamin D supplement, or eat plenty of oily fish, nuts and seeds and take plenty of sunlight

+ Eat a diet high in vegetables and fruit, especially blueberries, red goji berries, mangoes, papaya and wholegrains. These are all low in saturated fats and help maintain a healthy weight.

+ Eliminate sugar, processed and refined foods from the daily diet

+ Beta-Glucan supplements are an excellent immune booster. Porridge oats are a source of beta-glucan or you can take a supplement. Professor Gerbon of Humboldt University, Berlin says:

"As yeast has virtually disappeared from today's diet , since it has been replaced by chemical surrogates in the baking of bread, cakes and beer brewing, a daily intake of half a gram of beta-glucan can help prevent flu virus infections"

+ Spirulina is an excellent superfood and immune booster. Always buy organic, good quality with any health product.

+ Oil of Oregano Vulgare, (oil of Wild Oregano) is beneficial to boosting the immune system, is good for candida, antiviral, antibiotic, antifungal and antioxidant. It will kill any germ. Proof of this statement to be found in "Quarterley Review of Biology," March 1998, and "Indian Journal of Experimental Biology," June 1977. Take 1-3 drops three times a day.

- Relax before you eat to aid digestion

- Eat slowly and breathe deeply during a meal as this helps more oxygen enter the stomach. Do not rush meals

- Good "friendly bacteria" in the gut is destroyed by antibiotics and other drugs, so always take a good probiotic following a course of antibiotics, preferably for a few weeks to help replace the good bacteria. In "Science Daily" Dec 24. 2008, it states:

"Up to one in five people on antibiotics stop taking their full course due to diarrhoea. Physicians should help patients avoid this by taking probiotics, according to researchers at Albert Einstein College of Medicine. Antibiotics target good and bad bacteria".

- Enjoy your food, never feeling guilty if you have had the odd cream cake

- Drink plenty of water to stimulate the immune system, as it increases the white blood cells and flushes out toxins

- Eliminate an overload of parasites, which you may have if ill. Refer to section on parasites

- Lightly tap the thymus area, (upper chest, below the neck) with the fist for a few seconds as this stimulates the immune system.

- Laughter is an instant boost to the immune system, and helps with depression. In such cases, watch comedy programmes and surround yourself with fun people, to help lift your mood,

- A Rebounder, which is firmer than a trampoline helps to energise the immune system. Ten minutes on a rebounder is equal to half an hour brisk walking

- The properties of manuka honey were discovered by Professor Peter Molan, MD of New Zealand's University of Waikato. The higher the UMF, as discussed earlier, the more anti-bacterial properties. Research has proved manuka honey applied to ulcers on the legs can aid healing

- Taking Vitamin C 1000mg three times a day for a few months can also raise the immune system. Powdered Vitamin C is more easily absorbable.

- Garlic is a strong immune booster before, during and after cancer treatments. I recommend AlliTech from Dulwich Health. Allicin has been used to protect from MRSA, E-Coli, C-difficile, and other micro organisms

- Apricot kernels (rich in B17, also known as amygdalin), are excellent for cancer. Dr Ernst T Krebs Jr., biochemist, first produced laetrile (concentrated amygdalin), in the 1950s, and recommended a person eat 10-12 apricot kernels a day for life. See Phillip Day's book, "Cancer why we're still dying to know the truth," available from www.credence.org

- Plenty of Vitamin D, so exposure to the sun, for at least twenty minutes a day, will prevent ill health and boost the immune system. Even if there is no direct sun, fresh air, exercise and being outside will aid good health. If it is not possible to be out daily in sunlight and your immune system is low, take 5000 iu Vitamin D3 in droplets daily.

- An excellent immune booster is olive leaf extract, preferably taken in droplets.

- Mushroom extracts are an excellent way to boost the immune system and found to be contributory in healing cancer

- 11/22s as discussed in Chapter 3, using the statement, "I am healthy and well in mind, body, spirit,," or "My immune system keeps me in perfect health."

Body Cleanses

According to Miriam Young, www.detox4life.com.au it is very difficult knowing which organ to detox so she suggests the following as a guide:

Symptoms-Kidney Cleanse Program
Premature ageing
Lower back pain
Knee, hip problems

Symptoms-Colon Cleanse
Diarrhoea
Constipation
Fat, protruding belly
Mucous in bowel movements

Symptoms-Liver Cleanse
Liver disease
Fatty liver, high cholesterol
Cirrhosis
Hepatitis
Reproductive problems

Symptoms-Candida Cleanse
Reproductive Thrush
Vaginal itching
Hormonal imbalances
Infertility
Period pain
Endometriosis
Pre-menstrual tension, irritability

Digestive disorders

Symptoms-Heavy Metal Cleanse (Heavy metals such as mercury, aluminium, cadmium, arsenic, lead, tin and other metal poisons are present in our environment and invade our body)

Forgetfulness, frequent colds
Gastric problems, headaches
Impaired concentration, hearing loss
Kidney damage, metallic taste
Muscle weakness, tingling in hands and feet
Depression, neurological problems

Gall Bladder Cleanse

Around twenty per cent of people will develop gallstones in the gall bladder at some point in their life, which can cause severe pain and many months of waiting for an NHS operation. According to Rolf Gordon, from Dulwich Health, it is estimated as many as three million people worldwide have carried out the simple, painless and inexpensive gall bladder flush themselves, with over ninety five per cent success and it only takes six days. Milk Thistle can help promote the production of bile in the gall bladder, helps gallstones by dissolving them, and gives the digestive system a boost when needed, as it can act as a mild laxative. It also helps with inflammation of the gall bladder, kidney and bladder. Miriam Young, medical herbalist says:

"If you suffer from digestive problems, PMS, constipation or diarrhoea, high cholesterol, back pain, depression, menopausal issues, asthma, headaches or chronic fatigue, the cause could very well be gallstones. Contrary to most people's belief most gallstones are formed in the liver and very few in the gall bladder."

Here is Rolf's gall bladder cleanse:

Method for Gall Bladder Cleanse

+ Five days prior to flush, drink two litres of fresh organic pure apple juice. The malic acid in the juice softens the gallstones and makes their passage through the bile duct smooth and easy. During the five days eat normally but do not overeat

+ On the sixth day, have no evening meal

+ At 9pm take one or two teaspoons of Epsom Salts, or Andrews Liver Salts dissolved in 30 to 60 ml (one to two fluid ounces) of warm water. This will widen the bile ducts, therefore making it easier for the gallstones to pass

+ At 10pm, mix half a cup, 120ml (four fluid ounces), olive oil with 60ml (two fluid ounces) fresh lemon juice. Shake vigorously and drink all down

+ IMMEDIATELY upon finishing the olive oil and juice, go to bed, and lie on your right side with your right knee drawn up towards the chin

+ Remain in this position for 30 minutes before going to sleep. This encourages the olive oil to drain from your stomach, helping the contents of the olive oil to move into the small intestine. Next morning the stones will pass. They will be grey yellow or green in colour, and soft like putty, varying in size from grains of sand to some as large as a thumbnail. You may have the urge to go to the toilet before the stones will pass. You will be unlikely to feel pain

+ If not satisfied with the results, repeat the process a few days later, or even double the dose of lemon juice and olive oil

- It is advisable to repeat after four or five years have elapsed

- NB: The apple juice can be diluted with water, and if you cannot tolerate apple juice, substitute with cranberry juice

- Alternatives to olive oil include cold pressed oils such as grapeseed or sunflower oil.

Liver and Fats

Many illnesses can indicate underlying problems with the liver. Problems that are caused by an imbalance in the immune system often improve with a cleansing of the liver to improve its function. Certainly digestive problems, allergies, skin rashes, arthritis, headaches can be helped in this way. The liver protects the immune system from overload.

If you are overweight and struggling to shed those extra pounds then kick start the liver into speeding up the metabolism.

Women on HRT will find they may gain weight, as the liver has to work much harder to deal with the hormones in HRT.

Those who have abused their bodies with alcohol or recreational drugs would also benefit from carrying out a liver cleanse.

Symptoms of mild liver dysfunction include coated tongue, bad breath, facial bloating and a general feeling of not being quite "with it."

The twelve "Vital Principles to Improve Your Liver Function" says Dr Susan Cabot, author of "The Liver Cleansing Diet" are:

1. Listen to your body. Although this message is repeated many times, listen to the body's messages. If not hungry don't eat, or eat a raw piece of fruit or vegetables, or drink a glass of water. Eat when you're hungry.

2. Drink plenty of natural filtered mineral water spread out throughout the day as whilst cleansing the liver, it also helps flush out toxins. There is a high incidence of Alzheimer's in people who do not drink sufficient water. Do not drink fluids with meals.

3. Avoid eating refined sugar in your diet.

4. Don't become obsessed with measuring calories and weighing yourself.

5. Avoid foods which may upset your system. If you have a weak digestive system, it may help to take a piece of something raw before your meal, such as piece of raw fruit or vegetables.

6. Always promote intestinal hygiene, as the liver must filter out any bacteria and viruses present in our food. Wash hands when preparing, cooking and eating food.

7. Do not eat if you feel stressed, as during these states your blood is diverted away from the intestines and liver to other areas of the body, resulting in abdominal bloating.

8. Eat organic produce, free from pesticides.

9. Obtain protein from vegetable sources as well as animal.

10. Choose breads from a good source, without additives and artificial chemicals. Omit butter or margarine, and replace with hummus, tahini or fresh avocado.

11. Avoid constipation by eating plenty of fresh fruit, vegetables, dietary fibre and water. Make your own muesli with oatflakes, oatbran, linseeds, sesame, sunflower,

pumpkin seeds, psyllium husks and lecithin granules (the latter helps lower cholesterol).

12. Avoid excessive saturated or damaged fats (any fat that is rancid, refined or hydrogenated (trans fat), as these harm the liver if eaten regularly.

Good and Bad Fats

These are the so-called essential fatty acids because they are necessary for good health and the body cannot manufacture them. They do not make you fat. The main culprits here are sugar and refined carbohydrates.

There are good and bad fats. Bad fats are saturated fats, found in red meat and dairy products and can increase the risk of heart disease. Good fats, on the other hand, or essential fatty acids (EFA), are found in nuts, seeds, sprouting beans, avocados and oily fish. You can grow your own sprouted beans very easily and they are full of life force, essential fatty acids and good nutrients:

Six simple steps to sprouting your own seeds:

1. For sprouting use any dried pulses, for example aduki beans, chick peas, mung beans, lentils, peas, or alfalfa.

2. Rinse well in a sieve.

3. Place in a glass jar or sprouting tray in a warm dark place such as an airing cupboard.

4. Three times a day rinse well and drain the water.

5. Once sprouted after 4/5 days bring into the light and wash well

6. Eat in salads, sandwiches, soup or on their own.

They help reduce inflammation and will alleviate dry skin, lifeless hair, depression, premenstrual syndrome, high blood pressure and fatigue. They also boost metabolism therefore helping weight loss.

Avoid hydrogenated fats at all costs found in margarines, hydrogenated vegetable oils and other food products. They alter our immune system, affect blood insulin function, interfere with liver enzymes which are necessary for detoxification, increase cholesterol levels and alter the essential fatty acids which we require for good health. In particular, be aware of the dangers of TRANS FATTY ACIDS.!

Cooking With Oil

Do not overheat oils, as chemical changes occur, creating harmful trans fats. These are more hazardous for the body than saturated fats and are implicated in their potential to clog arteries, leading to heart disease. Food labels, indicating the presence of hydrogenated vegetable oil, should be avoided! For this reason it is better to choose butter over margarine. Certainly do not re-use oil more than a couple of times and be aware that in fast food outlets oil is reheated and used over and over again.

Heated oil will be ready to use for cooking if a piece of vegetable or bread sizzles straight away on contact. Discard if the oil has started to smoke. Stir fries are good but do not have the oil at too high a temperature and take more time to cook through.

Ideally choose organic cold pressed unrefined vegetable oils, or organic extra virgin olive oil, and store away from the light. Avoid polyunsaturated fat such as sunflower oil as it becomes unstable when heated. Keep temperatures as low as possible and ideally bake, grill, steam or roast food instead of frying.

Sandra Kendrew

Cholesterol

Cholesterol is a soft, waxy, fatty substance that is found within the bloodstream and cells. The liver makes about 75% of the body's cholesterol, and the body will manufacture all the cholesterol it requires. It is also found in foods of animal origin such as meat, fish, shellfish, eggs and dairy products. It has been found that cholesterol in foods such as eggs or shellfish does not increase the amount of cholesterol in the body.

If your cholesterol is very high, you can lower with the following products Allow at least three months to take effect, and more than one product may be required:

+ Lecithin granules, (2-3 tablespoons on cereals), will keep cholesterol soluble and prevents it being deposited as plaque on the lining of the inner blood vessels

+ Vitamin C can be taken from 1000mg- 3000mg per day. It is a good antioxidant, but take with plenty of water

+ Niacin (B3) reduces levels of Low Density Lipoprotein (LDL) and triglycerides in cholesterol, but check with your practitioner as to the level to take

+ Curcumin, is a spice which helps the liver eliminate excess cholesterol

+ Garlic and onions can bring down the levels of cholesterol, preferably eaten raw, otherwise gently cook

+ Coenzyme (CoQ10) is an antioxidant and natural chemical compound that we make in our bodies, and consume in our diet mainly from oily fish, wholegrains and liver. Most people as they get older do not produce sufficient so a suggested intake of 60-100mg, once or twice a day in a food state as ubiquinol, not ubiquinone, then a maintenance amount of 30 to 60mg daily when your cholesterol level had dropped

+ If taking medication to lower blood pressure and high cholesterol, 15-25mg zinc a day can help but check with your doctor or qualified nutritionist for any contra-indications

+ Psyllium husks and oat bran can be put in cereals to help lower cholesterol

+ Red Rice Yeast has excellent success in reducing cholesterol, refer to www.normshealy.com

+ Plenty of exercise and fresh air, such as brisk walking several times a week

+ Reduce stress levels, one of the biggest causes of high cholesterol

+ Focused awareness, relaxation, tai chi, or meditation

+ Balanced healthy diet with plenty of fresh fruit and vegetables.

According to conventional medicine there are two types of cholesterol. We have High Density Lipoprotein (HDL), which is good cholesterol, and acts as a scavenger collecting excess cholesterol, carrying it back to the liver to be reused or turned into bile.

Low-density Lipoprotein (LDL) is the bad cholesterol, and according to conventional medicine may build up in the lining of the arteries, causing them to become narrower and less flexible. This condition is known as artherosclerosis. If a clot forms in one of these narrowed arteries leading to the brain or heart, a heart attack or stroke may occur.

Also making up the total cholesterol count are:

Triglycerides: High levels of this dangerous fat can be the result of eating too much sugar or grains. Also at risk are smokers, those who take little or no exercise, drink alcohol to excess and are overweight.

According to best selling author Dr Joseph Mercola:

"Lipoprotein (a), or Lp (a) is a substance made up from an LDL "bad cholesterol" part plus a protein (apoprotein a). Elevated levels are a strong risk factor for heart disease. This has been well established, yet very few physicians check for it in their patients"

Your Total Cholesterol Level is NOT a Great Indicator of Your Heart Disease Risk.

The aim is to have a high reading of HDL, then the ratio of total cholesterol to HDL (total cholesterol divided by HDL), will not be too high.

According to Ron Rosedale MD, who is one of the leading anti-ageing doctors in the United States, **Cholesterol is neither "good" nor "bad".**

"Notice please that LDL and HDL are lipoproteins-fats combined with proteins. There is only one cholesterol. There is no such thing as good or bad cholesterol.

Cholesterol is just cholesterol.

It combines with other fats and proteins to be carried around the bloodstream, since fat and our watery blood do not mix well.

Fatty substances therefore must be shuttled to and from our tissues and cells using proteins. LDL and HDL are forms of proteins and are far from just being cholesterol.

In fact we now know there are many types of these fats and protein particles. LDL particles come in many sizes and large LDL particles are not a problem. Only the so called small dense LDL particles can potentially be a problem, because they can squeeze through the lining of the arteries and if they oxidise, or turn rancid, they can cause damage and inflammation.

Thus, you might say that there is 'good LDL' and 'bad LDL'.

Also some HDL particles are better known than others. Knowing just your total cholesterol tells you very little. Even knowing your LDL and HDL levels will not tell you very much."

In the United States and the United Kingdom, there is a widely held belief that cholesterol is extremely bad for you. This myth needs to be explained, as Dr Rosedale points out:

"First and foremost, cholesterol is a vital component of every cell membrane on earth. In other words there is no life on Earth that can live without cholesterol.

That will automatically tell you it is not evil, in fact it is one of our best friends.

We would not be here without it. No wonder lowering cholesterol too much increases one's risk of dying. Cholesterol is also a precursor to all of the steroid hormones. You cannot make oestrogen, testosterone, cortisone and a host of other vital hormones without cholesterol".

Cholesterol is also required to make Vitamin D from the sun.

Statin drugs, given to lower cholesterol, work by inhibiting not only just cholesterol, but a host of other substances and are responsible for upsetting the delicate balance of the body. For example, statins deplete the body of Coenzyme Q10 (CoQ10), which is beneficial to heart health and muscle function, therefore patients should be advised to take a supplement in the form of "ubiquinol" whilst taking statins.

The brain is the most cholesterol rich organ in the body, and low levels of cholesterol may impair the function of nerves in the brain and could lead to mental health issues. Dr John Briffa www.thecholesteroltruth. com says:

"In one epidemiological study, the relationship between cholesterol levels and depression was assessed in a group of French men and women aged 65 or older. The assessment continued for 7 years. This study found:

- *In men, low levels of low density lipoprotein (LDL) cholesterol (supposedly 'unhealthy' cholesterol) were associated with an increased risk of depression*

- *In women, low levels of high density lipoprotein (supposedly 'healthy' cholesterol) were associated with an increased risk of depression."*

The study is not the only one to link low cholesterol levels with mental health issues. Dr Briffa also referred to a recent Spanish review of the evidence which said:

"It is shown that low cholesterol in serum are associated and related to different neuropsychiatric disorders. Lowered cholesterol levels seem likely to be linked to higher rates of early death, suicide, aggressive and violent behaviour, personality disorders, and possibly depression, and dementia".

Dr Malcolm Kendrick, in his book, "The Great Cholesterol Con," and also quoted in the Daily Mail newspaper in January 2007, says:

"A leading researcher at Harvard Medical School has found women don't benefit from taking statins at all, nor do men over 69 who haven't had a heart attack.

A massive long term study that looked specifically at cholesterol levels, and mortality in older people in Honolulu, published in The Lancet, found having low levels of cholesterol concentrations for a long time, increases the risk of death. This may be because cholesterol is needed to fight off infection, or may have other functions."

I have found with much investigation into cholesterol, on an energetic level, high cholesterol is linked to suppressed emotions, in particular anger and fear. My suggestion is to do the Emotional Transformation Process regularly, particularly with any anger or frustration issues that are brought up, and at the same time do the 11/22s as given in Chapter 3, maybe using a statement such as "I live in peace and harmony." Over the eleven days you should start to release some of the suppressed anger. If it hasn't helped, leave another week and try another affirmation. You can also try any of the other emotional clearing therapies discussed in Chapter 3, but ensure the practitioners are fully qualified. Most importantly live in the present moment consciously as much as possible.

Liver Cleanse

Before any dieting regime it is a good idea to boost the liver by detoxing to help its function and metabolism. Any digestive disorders, liver problems, allergies, hernia, breathing difficulties, high cholesterol, menstrual and menopausal symptoms, endometriosis, diabetes, heart disease, hormonal imbalances, osteoporosis, chronic fatigue, cancer and depression, can be related to gallstones in the liver. Once the function of the liver is improved, the immune system improves. The liver is responsible for removing toxins from the body, recycling hormones, blood formation, and is the only organ to pump out excess fat. Years of abuse with drugs, pesticides, preservatives, contraceptive pills, antibiotics and alcohol can cause many stones to form.

On an energetic level and in traditional Chinese medicine, emotions such as anger are stored here, consequently too much stress can cause a blockage of energy within the liver, resulting in liver disorders.

For a full Liver Detox Program consult a qualified herbalist. I recommend a simple liver flush, done twice a year, ideally spring and autumn, and whenever you feel you may have over indulged on food and drink. It gives a general sense of well being, and helps to prevent fatty deposits from forming along the arterial walls. If you find this difficult, milk thistle and dandelion tincture are good to take, but I do recommend the flush for kick starting a sluggish liver. The milk thistle with dandelion can be taken alongside for a few weeks.

Liver Flush Drink

For one person and to be taken on rising:

8fl. ozs (200ml) organic apple juice, mixed with the juice of half a lemon
8fl. ozs (200ml) natural spring water
1 clove crushed garlic
1 tbsp. of extra virgin olive oil
Piece of fresh root ginger, ½" square, grated (stops nausea, but if the liver is hot or inflamed don't use).

Drugs, chemicals, alcohol and hepatitis can cause the liver to inflame. Symptoms can be an elevation of enzymes released by the liver, jaundice, loss of appetite, lack of energy and chronic tiredness.

Method

1. Liquidise all ingredients until smooth.

2. Transfer to a glass and sip slowly.

3. Follow the flush half an hour later with 2 cups of dandelion tea/coffee, or a detox tea.

4. Do not eat for at least one hour, preferably leave until midday.

5. If you feel headachy or slightly nauseous, this is because toxins need to be flushed out, so drink plenty of water throughout the day.

6. Ideally cut out tea, coffee and alcohol when doing this flush.

This needs to be taken each morning on an empty stomach. Try taking for one morning only, then for 2-4 mornings, then aim to do for 7 days in a row but whatever you can manage will be beneficial.

Cleansing the liver is the most powerful way to heal the body after the parasites have gone. We all have a certain amount of parasites in the body but some people have an overload, leading to ill health.

Kidney Flush

A simple kidney cleanse can be made with six fresh, medium sized beetroots, washed and boiled in a covered pan, with two to three litres of water, for about an hour. Allow to cool. Start gradually over the next seven days drinking 1-4 cups of the cooking liquid per day. If very sick or elderly, take one cup per day for ten days. Over the next four days eat one of the beetroots and a quarter of the liquid. This can help dissolve kidney stones. The usual indications of kidney stones are extreme pain usually near the lower back, but can be anywhere in the abdomen, usually accompanied with perspiration and often infection. Your doctor can clarify this, and I would suggest contacting a qualified medical herbalist.

Colon Cleanse

A sluggish colon results in a sluggish body. If you are feeling bloated, with excessive gas, constipation, stomach pains, candida, bad breath or difficult bowel movements, then it may be worth considering a colon cleanse.

If you don't have much time then a product called Oxy Powder from www.thenha.co.uk, or Oxytech from Dulwich Health will help. Take before retiring, and eat plenty of steamed vegetables and fruit which are good for a sluggish bowel.

Candida Albicans

Candida Albicans is a type of yeast that lives in the body and antibiotics, birth control pills and other dietary factors may contribute to candida overgrowth. It flies in the air looking for somewhere to land and reproduce and human tissue like the mouth (thrush), vagina and digestive tract offer the perfect environment. It can cause mood swings, depression, headaches and other health issues. First eliminate sugar and yeast products from the diet and avoid antibiotics. Keeping an alkali diet will help.

Mike Robinson, author of "The True Dynamics of Life," recommends the herb Pau d'Arco for treating candida, which has active ingredients, mainly lapachol, quercetin and other flavonoids. It also helps to clear the chest of mucous and has anti-cancer benefits. For further information on results with this product see www.paudarco.org .

Heavy Metal Cleanse

Liquid Zeolite which works on the cells in the body will help draw out heavy metals and toxins. Keeping a healthy immune system and looking after the liver will aid the release of heavy metals and toxins.

Pineapple Cleanse

Liquidise a fresh peeled pineapple, and drink once a day for a week, the second week every other day, and third week twice. Then for maintenance drink the juice once a week. This is excellent for detoxing heavy metals. Bromelain found in pineapples is a digestive enzyme and will get rid of intestinal worms and parasites, dissolve liver stones, (an alternative to the liver flush). The fibre in the fruit also helps bowel movements.

Dry Skin Brushing

This is of benefit to everyone, so invest in a good quality natural thistle brush. Don't use water, use the brush on dry skin before a shower, as this helps remove dead cells. Brush from the feet upwards. This encourages the lymphatic system to drain waste materials away from your body tissue and also helps with breaking down cellulite!

Chapter 9

Breathing and Meditation

Breathing is living. We could possibly survive without water for a few days, and food maybe longer, but without breath we may not survive for longer than a few minutes.

As a healer and dowser I have found the majority of my clients only shallow breathe, and hardly ever breathe a complete and deep breath that fills the lungs and abdomen. Breathing is done subconsciously and we are not generally aware of doing it. Breathing consciously and with awareness brings us into the present moment, which is often followed with a deep full breath. This will energize and relax the body, as well as reducing the negative effects of the stress hormones, adrenaline and cortisol.

Deep breathing like this will also alkalise the body, helping digestion and brain function. Most importantly it lowers stress levels, aids relaxation and encourages deeper sleep. If you are feeling tired and stressed, sit quietly and focus on the breath for several minutes until you are feeling a sense of calm.

The deeper we breathe the more Chi, Prana or Vital Life Force enters the body, bringing us alive with a feeling of well being.

Both positive and negative ions occur naturally in the air. Today our environment has more positive ions than in the past, caused by high voltage networks, TVs, radio, computers, radiation, cigarette smoke, smog, harmful chemicals and toxins. This can cause the acid/alkali levels in the body to become unbalanced. Positive ions are also known as free radicals which can cause cellular damage. Free radicals are organic molecules responsible for ageing, tissue damage and certain diseases. They are unstable and try to bond with other molecules, destroying their health, causing more damage.

Antioxidants which are present in certain foods and supplements are molecules that prevent free radicals from harming healthy tissue.

Negative ions in the air are tasteless, odourless and invisible and in higher concentration in clean unpolluted air, such as near the sea, or on mountain tops. Negative ions increase the flow of oxygen to the brain, giving a feeling of well being and alertness. When breathed they produce biochemical reactions in the bloodstream that increase serotonin levels, help to alleviate depression and stress and boost energy. This is why, in these natural surroundings, we can feel so much more relaxed than being in a densely polluted city.

Healing Breath

Breathing can boost the immune system, but breathing consciously is an instant aid to calm. Try the following:

1. Sit down, spine upright and feet firmly on the floor, and close your eyes. Start by raising the shoulders up towards the ears, then move backwards, keeping them raised and relax down. Do this a few times to relax the shoulders.

2. Take a few deep breaths through the nose, into the chest and down to the abdomen (belly) so that it expands on an in breath, and flattens naturally on the out breath.

3. Repeat as often as you like throughout the day, especially when tired and under stress.

4. This can be done as a relaxation, preferably lying on the floor but not on a bed as this can send you off to sleep, although done just before sleeping, can aid relaxation. Tense the whole body from the feet up. Tense all the muscles for as long as you can comfortably hold, then

release. This will help ease a headache and can also help insomnia. If falling asleep is a problem avoid heavy meals, watching TV in bed, exercise, stimulants such as tea, coffee and alcohol for at least two hours before bedtime. Sleep without the light on.

5.   Repeat 2 and 3 several times.

Alternate Nostril Breathing

This method of breathing relaxes the body completely, allowing you to be more energised. It is very helpful for people who suffer panic attacks or are overstressed, with a busy mind as it calms the whole system down.

*   Sit upright with your spine straight

*   Place the thumb of the right hand on the outside of the right nostril, the next two fingers on the brow centre (between the eyebrows, as this helps balance and stabilize the hand), then the ring and little finger rest by the left nostril

*   Breathe in deeply through the left nostril, closing the right with your thumb. The breath can be held for a few seconds if you wish

*   Then close the left nostril with fingers and breathe out slowly through the right nostril

*   Breathe in through the right nostril keeping the left nostril closed. Hold a few seconds if you wish

*   Breathe out through the left nostril, keeping the right nostril closed

*   You can count on the in and out breath, at your own pace

+ Start with doing three rounds then it can be built up to twenty rounds, but stop if you feel dizzy at any time.

Kapalbhati Yoga Breathing Exercise

This is a highly energising breathing technique with many health benefits:

+ Sit in a comfortable position, either with legs crossed or on a chair with your spine upright

+ Take three deep breaths in to relax the whole body from head to toe

+ Rest hands gently on knees with thumb and first finger gently touching as this helps keep the energy flow within the body

+ Exhale sharply several times through the nose as you pull the abdomen in and out strongly towards your spine

+ When you start struggling take in a deep breath and repeat

+ Initially you may only be able to do a few sharp fast exhalations but with practise aim to build up to 50. Eventually you may be able to do 100 without becoming exhausted. You can always look on YouTube for a demonstration!

Benefits:

+ Energises the whole body

+ Detoxes the body

+ Releases stuck emotions

- Improves digestion

- Abdominal muscles are strengthened

- Increase of oxygen in the body and the blood is purified

- Cleanses the lungs and respiratory system.

Focused Relaxation

Focusing with awareness on various parts of the body will bring about a letting go and a deep relaxation. Relaxation is better done on the floor with a rug, mat or on a carpet, rather than a bed. If you can tape these instructions it will be helpful but with practise you will remember it.

- Breathe deeply 3 times into the body and release slowly

- Bring your awareness to the scalp, breathe, relax and let go. Go to the left eye then right eye and relax, nose relax, mouth relax, jaw relax, tongue let go, breathe and relax. If you clench your teeth allow the jaw to open slightly

- Bring your attention to the neck and swallow if you feel the need

- Then focus on the right shoulder, arm, hand, breathe and let go. Repeat with the left side

- Bring awareness to the chest, abdomen, pelvic area, back, spine, from top to bottom, buttocks, breathe and let go

- As you exhale feel yourself melting into the floor

- Focus on the right thigh, then the right knee and feel the weight of the body as you are relaxing more and more. Repeat on the left side

- Go to the lower right leg, the calves, shin and ankles and be aware of letting go. Repeat with the left leg

- Bring awareness to the right foot, the big toe, next toe, middle toe, next one and little toe, top of the foot and arches. Repeat on the left foot

- Scan the body to check if there are still some areas of tension. Become aware and release

- Spend about twenty minutes for a complete relaxation, then stretch and get up slowly.

Either of these breathing or relaxation techniques may be done as a precursor to the Emotional Transformation Process in Chapter 3, if under stress.

Meditation

Meditation is not a religious practice in any way, nor do you have to subscribe to a certain belief system or philosophy. It is not a hypnotic trance as you remain completely aware. In the East meditation is a way of life and it is part of life.

There has been a tremendous interest in meditation over the last few years. The majority of people simply use it for eliminating stress in their lives, others to increase their spirituality and focus. Ultimately whatever the reason, there is no doubt that this deep form of relaxation leaves the participant feeling at peace and energized.

The goal of meditation is gaining a state of awareness where the mind is free of thoughts, worries and you are in a state of *being*. This is completely letting go, surrendering, and living in the moment in peace and harmony. Meditation is a tool to reach this state and this can take a lifetime to master or a few seconds!

It is turning your awareness inwards and being still, if thoughts come in that is fine, but just observing them pass by, staying detached, observing without judgement and being completely present, (you have heard me say this plenty but hopefully you will remember!).

There are many different paths to meditation and some of the systems used are:

Sight: this is the use of a visual object such as a candle flame, e.g., a flower or an object. It is just a focus to allow the mind to still.

Breath: As discussed earlier, an awareness of the act of breathing is another way to focus the mind.

Sound: This is usually a repetition of a mantra (a phrase), or a prayer, the most common being, "Aum" or "Om."

Apart from the mind, the body also benefits from meditation as there is a slowing down of the pulse, lowering of blood pressure, decrease in the breathing rate, a fall in stress hormones, and the level of lactic acid in the blood drops which aids the immune system.

I have talked about suppressed emotions being stuck in various parts and organs of the body. Meditation can unblock these emotions bringing a renewed flow of energy.

True relaxation is not sitting watching TV or reading a book, which can of course be relaxing. Deep relaxation is about releasing stress and letting go. The mind may wander, but is not in control - a pleasant state to be in, and can be used as a precursor to meditation.

Meditation is moving beyond the thinking mind, still alert and focused but moving into a deeper more profound state of awareness. Whilst meditating you become more mindful and conscious.

Meditation Using Visualisation

Visualisation is a tool to help achieve the meditative state. The Healing Breath in the previous chapter can be used as a precursor to any form of meditation.

Candle Meditation

+ Sit with your spine upright either on a chair or on the floor, whichever is comfortable

+ Place a lighted candle about 4-6 feet away, where you can see it clearly, (it may help to place on a table so that it is at eye level) but whatever is most comfortable

+ Gently gaze at the candle flame, noticing at first its outline, its shape, how it flickers, the colours of the flame, breathing and just noticing for a few minutes

+ Close your eyes and focus on the image you can see of the candle flame. How clear is it?

+ Gradually this will start to disappear, so you can repeat the procedure of gazing at the flame if you wish, or simply just visualise the flame with your eyes closed

+ With practise the image will become clearer and you can hold onto it longer. To end, open the eyes and take a deep breath in, whilst gently stretching the body

+ Using the candle flame as a focus is excellent for calming a very busy mind.

For a mantra meditation simply chant your mantra on an out breath, aloud or quietly to yourself. Allow twenty minutes for meditation, ideally twice a day, but ultimately five minutes is better than nothing.

Long term meditators have been found to age less than non-meditators. Using standardised methods of ageing, (eyesight, hearing and blood pressure), scientists found those who had been meditating for more than five years were physiologically nearly twelve years younger than their true age.

Meditation as a Way of Life

In our stressful society taking time to do any form of meditation is excellent. Ultimately we do not have to sit in a chair, on the floor or close our eyes. This is an excellent way to go within, calm ourselves, and be in touch with our inner being, but what happens after the twenty minutes of meditation? We go back to our daily business, and the stressful life we sought respite from.

The secret is to find a way of living in this state of bliss all the time, of living in the present moment, unaffected by whatever happens around us.

As explained, meditation is still an important way to focus and connect to intelligence, allowing healing to take place. When we are still and in a quiet place, it changes our vibration, and that of everything around us, and dissolves stuck belief systems. When in this void we can connect to intelligence or intuition, and maybe ask for guidance with a particular problem. If the answer doesn't come straight away, it may appear later in a magazine or on the television or just pop into your head.

When we learn to be still, intelligence or the universal life force flows through our being and elusive answers can be found. On the other hand, being stressed all the time blocks this natural flow of energy.

You can have a walking meditation, as long as you remain aware and in the moment of everything around you - every noise, flower, tree, building, car or anything else you pass. Use all five senses. It is ideal if done in the countryside as the chi/energy in nature is also cleansing and there is usually less pollution. Ultimately with practise you are able to meditate anywhere, whether on a bus or walking in a city. The important thing is to be aware of who and what is around you, being present, observing and NOT thinking about the past, or what you're having for dinner that evening or the following week. We all have to plan, but when the planning is done, come back into being mindful.

Gardening is an excellent way to be present. Be conscious of the flowers, weeds, notice the insects and just observe. This all takes practise but will change your life! If you don't have access to a garden, you can still be mindful when you iron shirts or peel potatoes! Focus on every action you do, the colour of the shirt you are ironing, and how the fabric feels.

When we are mindful and focused, this is when intelligence or intuition flows through, and we become more in tune with the flow of life. I personally find it hard to sit and meditate, so this was a revelation for me when I realised I could be mindful anywhere, at any time.

We all benefit from slowing down our busy thoughts, but as individuals we have to choose which method resonates with us. If you are an avid meditator, that is brilliant, practise regularly, ideally in the morning, and evening, or whenever feels right. Also try making small changes to your daily life. Walk more slowly, stop rushing, breath deeply and start noticing what is around you. When you go into town start noticing what you pass on the way to your destination. Be aware and be conscious!

Mindfulness is listening with full attention, and by doing this you are engaging all five of your senses and removing any judgements, attitudes or beliefs that can influence your perception of life. It is about feeling and experiencing each moment.

When constantly worrying about the future, your health, and finances, you ignore the world that is flowing by you, because your energy is somewhere else. Mindfulness means you adopt a life without ego, letting go, accepting what happens and trusting your higher intelligence.

These Mindfulness exercises are taken from Lynne McTaggart's course,
"Living The Field":

- Use mindfulness in every ordinary situation-when preparing dinner, brushing your teeth, be aware of the smells, textures, colours and sensual feelings you are experiencing

- Learn to really look at your partner, children, pets, friends and work colleagues. Observe every part of them closely during every activity-without judgement

- Learn to observe situations like noise, chaos and stillness without judgement. Notice the colour of the day, the light in the room, the movement carrying on in front of you, the sensations of quiet

- Cultivate the art of listening to all sounds: the rumble of a pipe, honking of a horn, barking of a dog, an aeroplane flying overhead. Listen to what your life sounds like. When someone speaks to you, hear the sound of their voice as well as the words. Don't think of a reply until they have stopped speaking

- Whenever you catch yourself judging what you see, think "I am thinking" and return to observing with simple attention

- Try not to try. Work on stopping your expectation or striving for certain results. This doesn't mean not doing your work properly, but ceasing your expectations and anxiety over results

- Accept all that happens without judgement. This means putting away all opinions and interpretations of what goes on. Catch and stop yourself from clinging to certain views, thoughts, opinions, preferences, and rejecting others. Accept your own feelings and experiences, even the unpleasant ones

- Try never to rush. If you must rush, be present in the rushing. Feel what it feels like

- Stop comparing yourself to anyone

- Don't think about or try to work out your problems. Just deal with whatever daily problem solving is immediately in front of you. As writer Flannery O'Connor put it, "Everything that rises shall converge."

Exercise

We are all aware of the need for adequate exercise, but can often find excuses not to do it. Not everyone has the time or finances to join a gym. As long as you are relatively fit, I suggest five times a week doing a very brisk walk for at least thirty to forty five minutes, (or whatever you can achieve), ideally in nature. Doing moderate exercise such as cleaning the house or gardening is also excellent, and even better if you can reach an aerobic state of being slightly out of puff'.

If you have health problems check with your GP before doing any exercise routine. By being in the fresh air, you are cleansing and revitalising your energy, obtaining Vitamin D, and if it is a power walk, which you should aim for, (suited of course to your age and health), then you are getting aerobic exercise.

Exercise can boost the immune system, allow more oxygen into the body, which helps with alkalising the blood, regulates hormonal levels and stimulates the body's natural feel good chemicals- endorphins- as well as improving mobility and flexibility. Make sure all exercise is Conscious Exercise, as you are more likely to lose weight this way.

If you have learnt the art of dowsing, as described in the next chapter you can check what is the best form of exercise for you, how many times a week you should do it and for how long. Otherwise be guided by your intuitive feelings and what you are drawn to. There is absolutely no point in joining a gym or going to an exercise class which you hate, as this can only do more harm.

For those less mobile, or anyone wanting to improve their posture, core muscles or just keep fit, Pilates is excellent. Choose a fully qualified teacher.

Yoga and Tai Chi/Qi gong are some of the oldest meditative physical exercises and excellent ways of keeping mind, body and spirit fit. Do not underestimate the effect these practices have on the body. Holding postures in yoga can be extremely aerobic! If you are someone who is highly stressed this form of exercise and relaxation is more beneficial and will become a way of life!

The websites I recommend are www.springforestqigong.com www.cloudwater.com and Kim Eng at www.Eckhart Tolle.com who has a DVD called Qi Flow Yoga.

I like to get my energy flowing and rebalancing first thing in the morning by doing the following:

Energising the body

- Stand hip width apart, stretching the spine and standing tall

- Relax the knees, shoulders and take in three deep breaths

- On each exhalation relax the whole body from the top of the head to the toes

- Pull the shoulders up to the ears, round to the back and relax, three times

- Start with the right arm and shake vigorously, visualising all the energy within it being stimulated, rebalanced and awakened

- Then shake the right leg, really allowing the energy to move

- Repeat with left arm and leg

- With the feet on the ground, shake the whole body for a few minutes, as hard as it feels right, just listen to the body and move how you want

- On an outbreath release any sounds as loud as you wish, this helps move your energy, and stuck emotions.

- Slowly come back to standing, take in 3 more deep breaths and relax. Feel the body you will feel more energised and alive

Finally, for the elderly, or anyone who has limited movement, there is no escape! Research has been done into whether visualising exercise is as productive as actually exercising, and to my delight the results are staggering!

A recent study by Erin M. Shackell and Lionel G Standing at Bishop's University Canada, revealed, you may be able to make the same gain in fitness as those who exercised, by simply thinking and focusing on a workout and just laying still!

The study measured the strengths in three groups. The first group did nothing different outside their usual routine. The second group went through two weeks of highly focused strength training, three times a week. The third group listened to audio CDs which used guided visualisations the same as the exercising group. Guess what happened?!

The first group who didn't do anything saw no gain in strength, the exercise group who trained three times a week, saw 28% gain in strength, and the third group who just visualised themselves exercising saw 24% gain in strength. Quite incredible!

You can read more about this report on the internet www. mindpowernews.com. It certainly shows we are more powerful than we realise.

Chapter 10

The Art of Dowsing

"We may think of it as a vast, hidden database of human awareness, which is characterised by powerful, universal organising patterns. Such a database, comprised of all the information ever available to human consciousness, implies stunning inherent capabilities; it's far more than just a giant storehouse of information awaiting a retrieval process. The great promise of the database is its capacity to 'know' anything the moment it is 'asked', for it is able to tap in to all that has ever been experienced anywhere in time."

David R. Hawkins, MD, PhD Director of the Institute of Advanced Theoretical Research on collective consciousness, taken from Elizabeth Brown's book "Dowsing," who goes on to say:

"We are all interconnected expressions of a collective whole. Everything is consciousness. And all consciousness communicates. So get used to the idea that we are all consciousness and therefore we all have the ability to communicate with everything that has consciousness. All we need is a means of access. And that is where dowsing comes in."

Definition

The art of dowsing, whether using a hand held V rod, Angle rods, or pendulum, is to search for that which is hidden or unseen. Traditionally it has mainly been associated with finding underground water or oil but nowadays has many more uses.

History

There are many claims of reference to early cave drawings from 8000BC, with a forked stick, but many of these are unsubstantiated. According to The British Society of Dowsers website:

'In 1556 Georgius Agricola published his work "De Re Metallica'" which clearly shows dowsing activity. One dowser is shown cutting a tree, whilst two others are in the act of dowsing using forked twigs, whilst surrounded by miners digging.

During the nineteenth and twentieth centuries dowsing for water to mark the spot for drilling wells and boreholes was a well established practice, with exponents such as Mullins and Tompkins combining their practice as dowsers, with the business of well drilling, frequently offering their services on the basis of 'no water no fee', so confident they were in their abilities.

During the twentieth century dowsing organisations began to be formed with the French Les Amis de La Radiesthesie founded in 1931, whilst this society was founded two years later by Colonel A H Bell OBE, DSO, MRI.

Since then societies have been founded all over the world, expanding the knowledge. The true value and worth of dowsing can be verified by the track record of successful dowsers."

The majority of practitioners carry out dowsing according to a code of ethics, and always for the highest good of all concerned. Unfortunately a few people and some religions, through fear, think it is something sinister, as Elizabeth Brown in her book "Dowsing-The Ultimate Guide for the 21st century" explains:

"However in the past 500 years dowsing has gone through periods of relative respectability. Dowsing was helped enormously by Queen Elizabeth 1 later in the 16th century. She was keen to introduce mineral dowsing to England to keep pace with the commercial success Germany had."

How can anything used for the benefit of the planet and mankind, bringing harmony and giving people their lives back, be in any way wrong? We are in the 21st century not in the dark ages where people were burnt at the stake through fear and ignorance.

The former Soviet Union, one of the more advanced countries in its attitude to dowsing call it "biolocation engineering", and four scientific institutes run annual courses to train students as part of the geology, mining and hydrology curriculum.. One of the country's leading experts in dowsing, Professor Alex Dubrov has reported that Soviet dowsers have had a 90% success rate in finding water, and 87% success in finding mineral deposits such as gold, oil, silver and platinum.

Dowsing is only a tool, and in my understanding, an inner process, connecting the conscious with the subconscious-a bridge between matter and spirit. Another simple way to understand the process is to think of the left side of the brain asking a question. The dowser becomes quiet and still, allowing the right side of the brain to answer. Dowsing is one of the many methods to connect to the intuition, and the one I find to be most beneficial in strengthening the connection.

Life has become something of a maze. Which diet? Which food? Which pills? Conventional or complementary medicine? Which therapist? Those who are good at connecting to their intuition or gut feeling find it easy to go with it, but most people struggle, and then doubt their choice, so dowsing can save us time and money.

Can Anyone Dowse?

The answer is yes, some have the ability to learn more quickly than others, but with perseverance anyone should be able to do this. Being still and unattached to the outcome is the secret and a skill in itself, but can be learnt. In Lynne McTaggart's "Living The Field" course she quotes from Christopher Bird's book "The Divining Hand: 500 year old mystery of Dowsing" where he says:

"According to experiments by Dr Zaboj Harvalik, a physicist and scientific advisor to the US Army, virtually anyone can dowse. In the 1960s he tested the ability of ordinary people to detect a buried wire through which a variable electric current could be passed. Using dowsing rods similar to

the L shaped coat hanger variety, 80% of the people Harvalik tested were able to detect a tiny milliamp current-with some even responding to as little as half a milliamp. (A 100 watt bulb draws less than 1 amp of current; 1 milliamp (a thousandth of an amp) is the smallest current you can sense, producing a buzzing feeling if it passes through your skin)".

It is important to be in the right frame of mind before you dowse. A relaxed and positive attitude is imperative. Avoid trying to prove anything to sceptics. When you have dowsed for a long time with successful results as I have, you don't need to prove yourself. You know it works. As long as it is remembered at all times that you dowse for the highest good of all creation, and not for the winning lottery numbers, tempting as it is!!

It is my understanding that the subconscious mind sends signals along the neurological pathways that control the movements of the pendulum or rods in the desired direction. So when someone says to me that they saw me move my hand, then yes, they probably did, but I am certainly not forcing the tools to move in a certain way.

The British Society of Dowsers has many recognised tutors, and I have found them to be an immensely helpful group of people for those wishing to further their knowledge. For dowsing courses throughout the country go to www.britishdowsers.org

For those who have difficulty going to courses or short of time I offer online courses, so refer to my website for information www.thehousehealer.co.uk There is an American and Canadian Society of Dowsers and groups in many other countries. See the reference section for more information.

Dowsing may be an ancient art, but it is on the cutting edge of science and new discoveries in physics are classing it as this. Dowsers are employed by many institutions worldwide. Water boards carry dowsing rods in their vans. The armed forces such as the US Marine Corps in Vietnam used dowsing to detect underground mines and

American Intelligence have used dowsing to locate missing planes and uncover hidden drugs, to cite just a few examples.

Uses

- **Water-** a good dowser can predict where there is underground water, as well as the depth, volume and pressure

- **Archaelogical searches-**dowsers are able to detect changes in soil formation beneath the surface and to find hidden foundations of early buildings

- **Soil testing and agriculture-**soil can be analysed for acidity, organic content and nutrient status. Plants and animals can be checked for diseases and germination

- **Mineral and oil prospecting-** dowsers have located minerals for many years, and the use of dowsers to locate oil wells is also well documented

- **Site surveys-**can be used to locate hidden and dangerous mine shafts, underground tunnels and other building services

- **Healing and medicine-**dowsing is successfully used to detect the causes of inbalances in a persons health, as well as finding suitable remedies, allergies, food intolerances, as well as rebalancing the body

- **Earth energies and geopathic stress-**the study of the energy patterns associated with standing stones and other ancient sites, can be assisted by dowsing. These energies interact with modern buildings and the people who dwell in them, especially if they sleep or work in geopathic stress and other non beneficial energies. These can be found and rectified through dowsing. Further information can be found in the next chapter

+ **Missing people and objects**-although a difficult area for many dowsers much success in this area has been reported. For further information on this, contact www. britishdowsers.org

Tools and Equipment

The instruments and tools dowsers use are very simple, and an extension of the human response, giving a clearer signal than can be detected without them. The tools act as a link between the dowser and their subconscious mind. There are many different tools which can be purchased from the British Society of Dowsers website, but these are just a few.

+ **V Rod**-Traditionally this was a forked twig, generally hazel or willow were chosen for their flexibility. Nowadays we use a springy material such as wood, cane, plastic or metal

+ **Angle Rods**-These are L shaped rods, usually used in pairs. Can be made out of a metal coat hanger. When the target is reached the rods will cross

+ **Wand**-This is a single long rod held in the hand, and will react with circular or oscillating movements

+ **Pendulum**-This is an object suspended from a fixed support, so that it can swing freely back and forth under the action of gravity, and is often used in conjunction with charts, or over a map for distant dowsing.

Device-less Dowsing

There are many methods used under this section, some experienced dowsers do not need to use a standard dowsing tool. Instead they listen to their bodies, which have become highly tuned receivers, not requiring an aerial link to tune in. The ones I use are:

- **Chain Link**-firstly, pinch the thumb and fingers together on each hand. Now open slightly and link together, so the finger and thumbs of each hand are forming a link like a chain, and locked firmly. You then become very still, calm, breathe deeply and detach from the mind. Say to yourself, "show me a yes response." You will find either the fingers stay locked and don't part, or they may separate easily as you pull away. My "yes" response is where the fingers stay locked, and "no" response, the right finger and thumb stays closed but the left opens easily to allow the right to glide through. This is excellent if you are in a supermarket checking out which food you should buy, as bringing out a pair of dowsing rods or pendulum will look ridiculous!

- **Whole Body**-One method is to use your arm as a pendulum. Stand upright, then lean to one side so that the corresponding arm is swinging loosely as if your shoulder is dangling from a piece of string. Ask your arm to give a "yes" response, then a "no" response and see what happens. Again this can be used as a discreet method of finding an answer, without being publicly visible! Another method with the whole body is to stand upright and ask, "'show me a "yes" response," where the body will move slightly forward, and for a "no" response, move slightly back, or vice versa. Whatever answer you get is right, go with it. And if nothing happens, practise, and practise. If this isn't the way for you, don't give up, but try another method.

Prior to Dowsing

When starting to dowse it is important you protect and rebalance your energy, and allow the mind to be still. You can follow the exercise in Chapter one to allow yourself to become very peaceful and calm, or follow one of the meditation or relaxation exercises given in the previous chapters.

Some experienced dowsers just take three deep breaths to centre themselves and off they go. With experience you will know which way is best for you, but I cannot emphasise enough the need to be calm and relaxed with a detached mind to perform dowsing to the best of your ability. It took me nearly a year to build up confidence and trust in myself, so if you don't get the correct answer to start with, do not give up, try and try again.

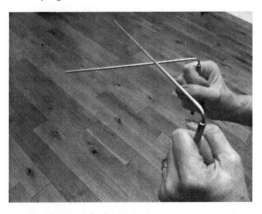

Simple Dowsing Method With L-Rods
(from the British Society of Dowsers)

1. This example uses two angle rods, which can be simply made from a pair of metal coat hangers, cut appropriately and bent into a right angle. The short arm of the L is placed in the closed hand with just enough pressure to allow the long arm to swivel, but not to wave about uncontrollably.

Some people prefer to place the short arm (which you hold in your hands), inside a tube such as that obtained from an old ball point pen, or a straw cut down to size, allowing the rod to move more freely.

2. Before I start dowsing whether it is using a pendulum or L rods, I always ask "Is it appropriate for me to work with whoever or whatever."

3. Getting a "yes" or "no" response will require some patience and perseverance. With some people it is instant, others may take a little while. Just ask the rods to give you a sign for "yes," and they may move inwards, outwards, or nothing may happen. Then ask the same for "no," which should have a different response. If you are struggling, maybe leave it until another day, then ensure you are completely relaxed, and try again. If you really struggle try using a pendulum instead as explained below.

4. The long arm of the rods are held parallel to the ground and parallel to each other as the dowser walks forward over the search area.

5. It is important for the dowser to have a clear mental focus on that which is being sought.

6. When the site of the target is reached, typically the rods will swing together and cross. The spot can be marked.

This can be checked by walking towards this point from the opposite direction. If the target lies along a line, such as an underground water pipe or stream, the action can be repeated to the right and left of the original search with markers being laid down on the ground to indicate the run of the line.

7. Alternatively the run of the line can be followed, holding the rods as before, when it is likely that the rods will move to the left if you walk to the right of the line or right if you walk to the left.

8. Occasionally other dowsing signals will be given and most experienced dowsers can interpret their own signals in the light of experience

9. The depth of the target can be determined by using what is known as The Bishop's Rule. Having established the site of the target, the search mode is again adopted and the dowser walks away from the target until the rods cross again. This can be checked by walking away in the opposite direction. The distance from the target to where the rods cross is equal to the depth underground. Obviously there are no limits to this technique depending on the nature of the terrain

10. There are more sophisticated dowsing techniques which can be learnt, either from the BSD or my online courses

Dowsing using a pendulum

1. When choosing a pendulum (a small weight on the end of a four-ten inch piece of thread, string or chain), it doesn't have to be an elaborate or expensive one. A past President of the British Society of Dowsers, Dr Patrick

MacManaway, simply uses a bolt on a piece of string. Equally you can use a set of car keys, although this may be for more experienced dowsers! Pendulums range from silver, brass, stainless steel or crystals. Look on the BSD website where they have a huge selection of dowsing tools, or refer to my website.

2. Before dowsing with the pendulum, relax and calm yourself as you did with the L rods.

3. Hold the pendulum where it feels comfortable and just allow it to swing back and forth very gently. To start dowsing from a still pendulum is very difficult when you are just a beginner. Once the momentum is going and your hand is still, ask the question, "give me a yes response." See which way the pendulum moves, initially it may only go very slightly in one direction. Once you have a discernible response, repeat asking for a "no" response.

4. With patience and practice you should get two different responses. The ideal is to have a "yes" moving clockwise and "no" anticlockwise, but any difference is absolutely fine. Once you are confident, you can ask for a "maybe" response.

5. Initially keep the questions simple, "Is my name Catherine?" Then, "Is my name Peter?" Once you start dowsing for other people always ask is it appropriate to dowse today for whatever, or whoever.

6. As you become more proficient try this exercise with a friend; have three cups, and put a different object under each cup, then ask the friend to find which object is under which cup. Dowse for which food/drinks/vitamins/pills are good for you.

7. Draw a half a circle then divide into ten segments, marking 10%, 20%, 30% up to 100%. Now hold the pendulum in the lower centre of the chart and ask: (a) How healthy is my diet? (b) How healthy is my energy? The pendulum will start swinging towards one of the percentages. There is an excellent book, "The Pendulum Charts" by Dale W. Olson, but you can easily make your own charts. If you are a homeopath for example, you can dowse the list of remedies for a patient.

8. Initially keep the questions very simple and have fun!

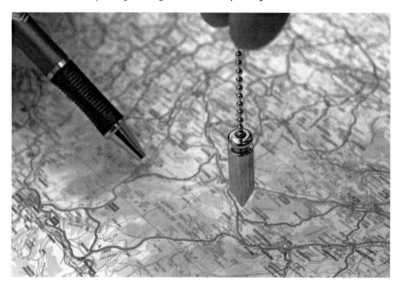

Focusing with Intent

The ability to focus with intent on whatever you are looking for, and keeping the mind still, is the key to dowsing success. It is necessary to remain completely detached for whatever you are dowsing and then trusting the outcome. Do not allow the mind to creep in and influence the answer. Once you ask a question, keep the mind out of the way, just breathe and relax, then wait for an answer. If you become a Doubting Thomas as I did in the early days, it will hinder your progress.

If you are searching for unbalanced energies within a property, you must keep your focus on unbalanced energies, then the rods/pendulum will direct you.

If you struggle with the mind influencing the answer, get two pieces of paper and write on one "yes", and the other, "no", then fold them up, place on a table, so you do not know what is written inside. Then with your dowser, ask the question and hold over each bit of paper saying, "Is this the correct answer?" and trust what comes up.

Always ask straightforward questions which will have a yes or no response. Long complex enquiries will not give you a very accurate or satisfactory answer.

Witness

Some dowsers like to use a "witness" or sample of what they are looking for. A health dowser for example, may ask for a sample of hair, or someone dowsing for minerals, may have a sample of a certain mineral at the end of the rods. I personally don't use this method as I explain in the next chapter.

General

Dowsing can be extremely draining and I recommend drinking plenty of water. When you are starting, dowse for no more than an hour, then build up to maybe a couple of hours. I often dowse for up to three hours, but have to be careful not to exhaust myself.

Do not get into a habit of dowsing for friends' personal or health problems, unless very experienced, but even then always ask if it is appropriate to do so.

With practise you will find yourself drawn more to one area of dowsing than another. You may prefer to specialise in dowsing for health or dowsing for underground water, earth energies, or map dowsing for non beneficial energies. Some people dowse to find missing objects or people. You may be better suited to one rather than another, so do not lose faith if you can find underground water, but not a missing object.

Do not allow the ego to enter into your dowsing, as you may find you will take a fall and possibly be very humiliated. Just remember, it is not you giving the answers, it is something much greater inside you, so always show gratitude at the end of the dowsing for the help you have received.

It is a tool to connect the subconscious and conscious mind but the ultimate paradox is when you have truly discovered, mastered and trusted your dowsing, you will not need to dowse. You will have connected to the intelligence that flows through you. You will know yourself, the universe, and the truth of all that is. We are masters and creators of our destiny!

Chapter 11

Geopathic, Geopsychic and Electromagnetic Stress

Geopathic Stress

There are natural rays emanating from the earth which can be balanced, good energy or, because of earth disturbances, may be out of balance and can cause discomfort and ill health to anyone living above them or in their path.

Unbalanced earth rays go by many names such as black streams, cancer rays, negative green rays, Hartmann and Curry Lines, and even Ley Lines. Rolf Gordon, author of "Are You Sleeping in a Safe Place," just calls them Geopathic Stress, as I prefer to do.

The term "geopathic" is derived from the Greek word "Geo" meaning "the Earth," and "pathos" meaning "disease" or "suffering" so literally, "suffering of the earth."

Depending on the strength and character of the earth energies present, a location may carry beneficial energy, on the other hand it may be potentially harmful to some people.

Geopathic Stress is the earth's natural radiation which rises up and becomes distorted by weak electromagnetic fields created by underground water, certain minerals, fault lines, quarrying, construction, weather and earthquakes.

The earth like all living things has an energy field and is covered by a system of grid lines. Originally these lines produced beneficial balanced energy to the planet which enhanced optimum health.

When this energy field is disrupted the energy becomes non beneficial to our health.

Geopathic Stress does not cause illness directly but it lowers the immune system, increasing the risk of disease. Conditions implicated include: cancer, arthritis, rheumatism, asthma, migraines, insomnia, multiple sclerosis, heart disorders, post viral fatigue (ME), inflammations, sudden infant death syndrome, miscarriages, emotional and mental disorders and many other depleted immune system conditions.

If you or your family members are unwell, check your house is free from Geopathic Stress.

Since the inherent frequency of the earth is 7.8 Hertz (Hz) (known as the Schumann's Resonance), a person's brain waves also resonate with that same frequency, which is required for optimum health, but strong geopathic stress can vibrate as high as 250 Hz. Even though you may not have heard of geopathic stress, you will have felt the effects of it. We have all walked into a house and felt uneasy or very tired and lethargic in a particular room or building. On the other hand if you love being in a certain property it will often have good beneficial energy.

When rebalancing the energy of a property all living things have to be considered as some animals, plants and trees thrive in an area of geopathic stress. Some examples of those who seek and thrive on geopathic stress energy are:

Asparagus
Mushrooms
Mistletoe
Medicinal herbs
Oak trees
Fir trees
Plum and cherry trees
Elderberry

Sandra Kendrew

Cats (if they sleep on your bed this maybe an indication of geopathic stress, so perhaps not a good place for you to also sleep!)

Ants
Bees and wasps
Beetles
Termites
Parasites
Bacteria and virus

Those which do not thrive in geopathic stress, apart from humans are:

Roses
Sunflowers
Lilies
Begonias
Azalias
Cacti
Privet hedge
Red and blackcurrant bushes
Cucumber
Celery
Onions
Maize
Apple trees
Pear trees
Beech and ash trees
Lilac trees
Nut bearing trees
Dogs
Horses
Cows
Sheep
Pigs
Mice

Chickens
Birds (will not lay eggs in GS)
Fish (will not spawn in GS)

Nutrients will not be absorbed efficiently if your body is geopathically stressed.

Evidence Geopathic Stress Causes Illness

+ Baron Gustav Freiherr Von Pohl conducted the first documented study of the link between geopathic stress and cancer in 1929 and 1930 and found 100% correlation of earth radiation with homes of those who died of cancer. He proved to the Centre Committee for Cancer Research in Berlin that one was unlikely to get cancer, unless one spent some time in geopathically stressed places

+ This research was also confirmed by Kathe Bachler, an Austrian teacher and researcher, who studied over 11,000 cases of geopathic stress, mainly on schoolchildren

+ Dr Hans Nieper MD, world renowned cancer specialist, states 92% of all his cancer patients and 75% of his MS patients are geopathically stressed

+ Professor J. Graz MD recommends a change of bed position to those who do not respond to his medical therapy

+ Dr Ernst Hartman MD is convinced after treating thousands of cancer patients over thirty years of practice, that cancer is a disease of location caused by geopathic stress

+ Dr Hager MD found geopathic stress was present in all 5,348 cancer cases investigated

- Arnold Mannlicher MD thinks that cancer is a disease of location. He wrote in a Swiss medical journal that in thirty years of practice he has not yet found a case of cancer where there was an absence of influences from the earth

- Dr Rambeau MD says that a house built on neutral ground and still producing cancer does not exist.

Electro-Magnetic Stress

We are living in a world of man-made pollution, due to phone masts, pylons, underground and over ground cables, phone base stations, computers, mobile phones, WIFI, Bluetooth, microwaves and baby monitors. Refer to www.emfields.org for further information on this.

Dowsing for me has been an invaluable tool for identifying any electromagnetic stress in my home and surroundings as well as for clients all over the world.

There are many devices to attach to mobile phones to protect you from EMF but I would like to share one tip to minimise radiation. If you are dialling someone on a mobile phone, hold the device at least eight inches away from your head until the person at the other end has answered.

With telephones, the ideal would be to return to the old fashioned corded type but I appreciate that is not an option for most people. An alternative is the low emission phone and there is plenty of information on the internet on where to purchase. I suggest looking at www.powerwatch.org.uk a non profit making independent organisation, giving advice on avoiding electromagnetic fields and microwave radiation.

It is possible to purchase a dLan from Devolo, www.devolo.co.uk or Maplins electrical store, which can connect your Freesat box to your broadband, via the mains electrical sockets in your home, to minimise radiation exposure.

In the next chapters I explain in more detail in how I deal with electromagnetic stress in homes.

Schumann Waves

Schumann Waves were first discovered by Professor Schumann, a German scientist. They are naturally occurring beneficial electromagnetic waves of energy existing above the earth. They help regulate the body's internal clock.

If a building is constructed of concrete or has a metal roof, it can make the occupants lethargic or cause insomnia. Check the building you are working or living in. It is thought the reason why some people feel jet lag may be connected with the metal fuselage of an aeroplane obstructing beneficial waves of energy. Dr Ludwig, known as the Father of Magnetic Therapy, convinced NASA to install Schumann Resonance Devices on the spacecraft, for the health of the astronauts.

Grounding/Earthing

Our feet have more nerve endings than any other part of the body as any acupuncturist or reflexologist will tell you. We take in the earth's energy through our feet, so it is a good idea to go barefoot as much as possible. Footwear should have leather or hide soles. Plastic, rubber or composite soles do not conduct the earth's electric energy.

There is a market for a shoe company to make grounded shoes. Going barefoot will quickly restore your energy. I heard of a lady who had travelled the world and suffered terrible jet lag. After standing on some grass outside for approximately thirty minutes, she felt completely recharged. This is how quickly it can work. For more information

I recommend an excellent book called "Earthing" by Ober, Sinatra and Zucker.

Earthing sheets can be placed onto a bed to help with insomnia, anti-inflammatory diseases, chronic pain, stress and low energy levels, hormonal problems and other illnesses.

Dr Stephen Sinatra, an Integrated Cardiologist, with over thirty years in medical practice says:

"I regard Earthing, as the greatest health breakthrough in all the years of medical history"

So take those shoes and socks off and walk on the ground!

Geopsychic Stress

When I dowse for geopathic stress I incorporate searches **for** geomagnetic and geopsychic stress. The latter can very simply be unbalanced energies left from previous occupants in a property, or from present occupants. If you have a family who is constantly arguing, the expelled energy remains around the home and if not rebalanced, will cause more aggravation. I show people how to do this for themselves, once a property has been healed.

Constant negative thoughts within a property will cause non beneficial energy to linger and will not be advantageous to the occupants. Laughter will always lift the energy of a place!

I spoke recently with an estate agent in my home town who said they have homes they call "divorce homes" as every two to three years the property is back on the market. This may be due to the constant detrimental expelled energies from previous owners, which are not cleared, therefore remaining in the house, affecting successive owners, making them feel uneasy and wanting to sell up and move on, so the pattern repeats itself.

The land a house is built upon can also generate ill health. I recently rebalanced the energies of a property in Melbourne, Australia, where on a small estate, most of the occupants suffered ill health. When investigated it was found the houses were all built on an old Aboriginal burial ground. There was quite a bit of trauma surrounding this area which was experienced by the occupants. I am happy to say their health improved tremendously after the land and houses were rebalanced.

When I dowse to check a property I usually check the energy of the client. Some people can attract non beneficial energy within their auric field, which can be called an "an entity attachment." I have found if there has been a lot of trauma, drug or alcohol abuse a person's auric field becomes very open and, like a moth to light, can attract detrimental energy to their being. This may cause them to act out of character or become very negative and depressed in their outlook.

In the early days of dowsing I occasionally had a property that was not rebalancing its energies, until I realised the vibration of the fabric of a building can hold memory. In other words if the original builder was angry and negative whilst constructing the property, this anger can be held within the materials used in construction.

I had a very bizarre sounding case where a small girl could not sleep. She went to bed with her head against a chimney breast. I traced it back to the chimney builder who was dealing with a lot of trauma at the time and this had imprinted itself into the stone work. Believe it or not, when this energy was realigned she slept soundly the next day, with no further problems since.

These cases can sound unbelievable and I like to think I am very level headed, but the proof is when someone regains their health and this has happened time and time again, I don't doubt anymore!

The more I work in this field of energy the more I realise what powerful beings we are. Over the years we have lost our connection with nature.

Similar to the experiments Dr Emoto did with sending love or hate to water and then photographing how the cells changed, I decided to do the same with trees.

So, out in the garden, armed with my dowsing rods, I sent thoughts of hate to a particular tree. Through dowsing I found out the energy field was about two inches away from the tree trunk. Then I sent thoughts of love and appreciation for having a beautiful tree in my garden, rechecked the energy, and yes, to my pleasure, the energy field came out to around fifteen feet, so a huge change. Yes, you can talk to your plants and trees and they will respond!

I took this a step further last summer when visiting a friend's house which was plagued with wasps. I thought if you can communicate with plants, then how about wasps? I asked the energy or essence of the wasps to find somewhere else and to go away from this site if appropriate. Guess what, no more wasps! As long as whatever is done, is done for the highest intention of all concerned then that is fine.

Another area of my work is helping "earthbound souls" to move into the light. When most people pass, they do go to the light, but occasionally if a person has died traumatically, had no belief system, fearful that they may be judged or didn't believe in life after death, they may actually become "stuck," between the earth plane and astral plane. They may have even been attracted to you or your children's energy, and should be encouraged to move on, which they usually do.

Dr Alan Sanderson, MB, BS, DPM, MRCP, MRCPsych, a psychiatrist, later in life devoted much of his work to spirit release. He found many of his patients who were suffering from phobias, drug dependency, hallucinations, eating disorders, depression and other mental problems, had a spirit attachment, and once removed they made a remarkable recovery.

He went on to found the Spirit Release Foundation, which is run by medical and complementary practitioners. www.spiritrelease.com

The above information may cause some people to think this work should be left alone, or is in conflict with their faith. My answer to this is as long as any practitioner works from their heart with a code of ethics, improves the health and lives of others, gives reassurance to those who have lost loved ones, and gives help for the highest good of a client, this is valuable work, and certainly should not be "put down" or judged by anyone.

Lack of understanding and fear should not stand in the way of people benefiting from an improved state of being.

Chapter 12

Healing Yourself And Others

Energy cannot be created or destroyed, but can be transformed
Albert Einstein

Healing Yourself

It has become something of a minefield for people to negotiate the number of different healing courses and information now available on the market. What I have found over the years of healing is keep it simple. There is no need for elaborate rituals, or for the healer to walk around in purple flowing gowns. I remember rebalancing a property for a newspaper editor, and when she opened the door, remarked on how normal I looked! I was a bit taken aback and joked that "I had left the broomstick at home!" I didn't arrive looking like a 60's throwback, in fact if I can remember, I wore a dark suit. She did apologise and when she wrote about my work was very positive and said the process had made a big difference to her family's life.

We need to heal and balance ourselves before attempting to heal others. Always remember the healer does not heal others, the healing is channelled through him or her. It is the universal divine energy which flows through everything, and is directed with intent by the healer to where it is required, and used for the highest good of all concerned.

Intention is the invisible intelligence in the universe that we are all connected to.

There must be no ego in this at all. Sometimes you come across people who, without any judgement say, "Healing is a gift from god so why do you charge?" Yes it is a gift from God to heal, as is being a pianist, a professional footballer or a good cleaner. We all have to make a living, and money is an energy so healers should never feel guilty about accepting payment for healing work. It can be in exchange for something else or a token amount, but acceptance allows the flow of energy. Whatever you do in your life, do it with love and to the best of your ability.

It is becoming more accepted that we are energetic beings and extremely powerful, more powerful than we can imagine, so we need to use this energy wisely.

At a time when the world is seeking more economical and less harmful sources of power, what about harnessing this vast sea of energy around us?

When commencing healing practices we need to be in a state of inner harmony and balance. It is helpful to start by finding a quiet area in your home where you will not be disturbed. The idea is to look for a state of gentle meditation, as discussed earlier and focusing on a flower, candle or your breath, whichever feels right to you at the time. This is not about concentration, it is simply letting go and breathing calmly. Rebalancing and protecting your energy is important, and trust this is so.

Breathing is very important to calm the mind and harness the divine or universal energies we have around us. Think of a tree. It doesn't just rely on the nutrients it derives from the soil. Its vitality depends on breathing through its leaves. This is how its chlorophyll is produced. Trees and plants absorb the "sea" of energy around them. Similarly, we do the same and when we consciously breathe in this "sea" of energy, our vitality is much more abundant.

Healing our being, is working on ourselves spiritually, physically, emotionally and mentally. The Emotional Transformation Process, in

Chapter 3 which I recommend you photocopy for daily reference, will help with this. Refresh yourself with it now if you have forgotten.

We ultimately need to live in a place of love. Love Heals! Where there is fear there is no love, only ego.

We live in a society of "never enough time, too busy." Through my years of healing and working on my own energy as well as others, I have found the simplest, quickest methods are just as affective as long drawn out rituals, which people cannot even understand. As long as what you do or say comes from the heart it will work. As a dowser I am also able to dowse as to the effectiveness of our thoughts and healing. But you do not have to be a dowser - just trust and know it works.

I have devised a "Statement of Intent to Heal and Rebalance Energy." I found in both healing myself and others distantly, this effectively changes the energy from unbalanced to balanced. Clients who have chakras "out of balance," after saying the statement, will rebalance them, and this happens very quickly. With dowsing I check and it works every time. Obviously the client has then to work on why they have become unbalanced, and watch their thoughts, feelings and emotions. This process brings them into Conscious Living, which is our ultimate aim in life.

There is a definite difference between reciting the Statement of Intent without a great deal of feeling and saying it with 100% feeling. I dowsed the effectiveness of saying this Statement without much feeling and meaning, and it is about 55-60% effective, whereas with 100% true meaning and feeling, its efficiency can go up to 95%, so this speaks for itself.

Statement of Intent to Heal and Rebalance Energy

(this can be done for yourself or others)

The wording can be adjusted to suit your own belief system and what feels comfortable.

"With INTENT I ask the divine/universal healing energies to bless and protect me, and bring complete balance to my physical, mental, emotional and spiritual being, removing anything not for my highest good to where it belongs, bring back all my energy, recharge and re-align it as appropriate, with infinite love and gratitude. So Be It."

I suggest this is done on awakening and before going to sleep.

Healing Others

The Statement of Intent can also be done for others if you wish, as long as we incorporate "as appropriate," as this is not interfering with the other person's "highest good."

The most crucial asset a healer can have is an absence of ego. In the early days of my work I was too excited and desperate to see positive changes in clients, and became disappointed if nothing changed immediately. Over the years it became my understanding, as long as we carry out the work with unconditional love and compassion, to the highest of our ability, we then hand over the outcome to the universe, and trust what will be, will be, and certainly not judge others or ourselves.

I had to learn to overcome my lack of patience. I wanted something, to happen immediately and became frustrated if my plans didn't work out. Then I realised how we have to trust the divine plan. We have created our own reality, so acceptance is the key. If we are too impatient, ultimately it means we don't believe we can create what we want, and we lose faith in ourselves as creators.

Most of my work is done distantly. It really doesn't matter if a person is in the next room or next continent. Dowsing works equally well in both settings. Before healing others Jesus said:

Physician heal thyself

Then you can help others. When helping others through an illness, teach them to listen to their bodies. What is your body saying to you? Do not become reliant on a healer, as they are there to help and guide you on your path, but then you need to do the work yourself.

Some people like to go weekly or regularly, relax, and enjoy the healing process, but then carry on in their same old ways when back at home. If you become too reliant on a healer or therapist you are giving away your power and not taking responsibility for yourself. A good therapist will help by guiding you in self-healing. This is self-empowerment.

When I carry out a health/healing check I tune into the clients' energy field and dowse for the following:

+ Energy levels in the aura before and after healing

+ Chakras' energy

+ Is the cause of the problem spiritual, mental, emotional, physical or environmental? I have lists of underlying causes, once I establish where the problem is

+ Cause of illness and time of onset

+ Percentage of parasites in the body

+ Acidity/alkali balance

+ Absorption of nutrients in the body

+ Are thoughts or emotions creating the problem?

+ Energetic imprint (maybe from a past virus or vaccination)

+ Past life trauma (can still be carried into this lifetime)

+ Cord cutting (on an energetic level some people cannot let go of other people so need to break ties)

- Nutrition and diet. If you can dowse and want to find out allergies or nutritional deficiencies, you can obtain charts of foods and nutrients from the internet or books, and ask which is required

- What is required for healing to take place?

- Always check to see if there is anything else you have missed.

The reason many healers can alter the course of an illness is because when they are in a state of calm, they transfer love to the client and the body will rebalance itself. I am not talking about possessive love but a state of unconditional love, similar to what we feel with babies and young children. If you can look at an illness for what it is, accept it without judgement, the cells will change. If you want to help and heal anyone be in a state of calm and compassion, which will rebalance their energy and heal.

This may not be easy as we can become angry and self pitying, allowing the "why me" syndrome to take over. Love, is linked to the heart chakra and we are here to open and heal this centre. Studies from the Institute of HeartMath in California confirm how health improves with love in the human body. When we feel love, gratitude and compassion, the heart sends messages to the brain and secretes hormones to boost health and the immune system.

Be in your heart area at all times, listen and feel what the body is saying. Be with any illness, don't run away, suppress or pretend it isn't there by keeping yourself occupied at all times. Write out or say how you are feeling. Just be with it and accept one hundred per cent.

We are all healers but occasionally we do require someone else to assist us with an illness, such as an acupuncturist, osteopath or a surgeon.

Sometimes a person may die in the process of healing, but this will help them pass over and it is important that the healer does not think their work has not helped or becomes too attached to the outcome, otherwise the ego has won.

EACH AND EVERYONE OF US REFLECTS THE WORLD

HEAL YOURSELF THEN YOU CAN HEAL OTHERS

Reconnecting to nature will help us all to heal, allowing intelligence to flow back into our lives. Unfortunately we have become disconnected from the true meaning of life and need to allow love, not fear, to flow through our lives.

Prayer

The power of prayer with intent and focus is much more profound than just repeatedly chanting something you know off by heart, with no feeling.

If you go into the place of stillness, *just be*, without thought, remaining present, and quietly think about who, what, or where you want to heal, a powerful transformation takes place. This type of prayer goes beyond saying, *"Please God heal...."* You are going directly to source, where we are all connected. This is a place where healing and transformation can happen.

Rebalancing and Potentising Water

I have blessed food and water, asking either your higher self, the divine or universal energies to rebalance and re-energise it, which works incredibly well. I dowse its effectiveness before and after. Some healers work with spiritual guides and ask them to carry out the work, which is equally effective.

I use the following procedure to help potentise water. Draw a two inch circle on a piece of white paper, then draw three circles half an inch apart around this. Write in the middle of the paper whatever you wish to remove, for example if you have radiation in your body from a recent aeroplane flight, write in the centre, REMOVAL OF RADIATION.

Then place a glass of water in the centre. With Intent ask that the glass of water, when drunk will remove the radiation in your being. If you can dowse, ask how long you should leave the glass on the paper, ie: how many minutes, how many hours? Then drink it knowing and feeling it is removing any radiation within your body. If you cannot dowse, just leave for a couple of hours, or whatever your instinct tells you.

I have done the above with sugar pills purchased from a homeopathic retailer, when people have had addictions to certain foods, drinks, or cigarettes. Place on the paper with for example, REMOVE CHOCOLATE ADDICTION, then, dowse for how many pills to take, and for how long. If you cannot dowse, tune into your intuition and ask yourself, how many should I take?

When healing clients with arthritis, amongst other advice, I ask for the vibration of calcium carbonate to be removed from wherever the problem lies. All of this I have found successful and the clients are fully aware of what I am doing.

We must not underestimate the power we all have in achieving amazing results, as long as the code of ethics is followed, and everything is done for the best and highest intention for all concerned.

When healing, allow and know this energy is flowing through you, not from you, otherwise you would be extremely tired and depleted. There are many excellent books on healing. I recommend Barbara Brennan's, "Hands of Light" and "Light Emerging."

Ultimately follow your instinct on healing and do what feels right for you. Some people heal by just being with you and others drain your energy. A counsellor who is compassionate, non-judgemental, and speaks from the heart, will have better results than an angry, frustrated person, so choose your practitioner in any field conventional or complementary, wisely!

I know of doctors and consultants who may not be aware of their powers, but are exceptional healers because they do not act from a place of ego, and genuinely want to help heal. Once ego steps in the compassion is limited.

Chapter 13

Healing Property

After spending many years healing and rebalancing energy within clients, and being aware of detrimental energies within properties, I decided to embark on healing buildings. We have talked about non beneficial energies within properties and the effect it has upon homes. One of the first things I do is ask all my clients to clear out clutter. Clutters hoards detrimental energy and will affect your health. I suggested earlier setting a goal if you found it difficult to let go of your possessions. Remember what is without is within and vice versa, so a cluttered house will lead to a cluttered mind. Start with small amounts of clearing, otherwise you will overpower yourself and nothing will be accomplished.

There is a "genius loci"-a spirit of place. The original inhabitants of a region built their sacred sites on Ley Lines, or "vital energy lines" running through the earth over vast distances. The Romans built their roads over Ley Lines and this is why they are so straight. Lynne McTaggart, author of "The Field," and "The Bond," states:

"Early cultures like the Mayans actually prefigured many of these lines. New evidence shows that these ley lines may indeed exist as a result of geomagnetic activity in the earth's crust, or as accumulations of the electrical charge from groundwater seeping through porous chalk deposits, which is particularly prevalent in the UK. This type of charge accumulation can be redistributed and spill over into other sites on the ground, offering a 'moving target' for electrical discharges coming from the air, thus creating a moving line of energy. In the case of Stonehenge or the Pyramids in Egypt, the latest scientific evidence suggests they are sacred because the energy of the inhabitants coalesce at a site like an energetic whorl, and their use

over the centuries has invested them with that quality, we in fact create our own spirit of place, depending on its use over time"

In other words we impress our energy upon a place. So if you buy a property it will have the memory or energy of its previous occupants. When buying a new property rebalancing the energies should be a priority. Some builders in Germany and Austria actually provide the owners with a certificate to say their property is geopathic stress free.

I have often found current homeowners suffering a similar illness to the previous occupants so I find out the history of a property to establish if this is so. It doesn't make any difference to my healing work but will give an indication to what is happening.

When a client initially contacts me to check the energy within their property, it is usually because someone within the household is not well. I ask for an address and dowse to see if geopathic/electro-magnetic/geopsychic stress is present. If it is then there are various options available. If there is geopathic stress, I send a questionnaire and request rough floor plans of the property. From this I can map dowse for exactly where the non beneficial energy is within a property.

Ideally, I like to work on the property and its occupants, as one affects the other, and I need to establish if the property or the occupants are causing the unbalance. I have lists of electromagnetic, geopathic and geopsychic stress problems that may be causing unrest in a property. It can be phone masts, pylons, radiation, allergies, smoking, radon gas, lead water pipes, virus and bacteria from water, nuclear energy, underground/overground cables, MMR scanners, computers and fluorescent lights.

Everything is consciousness so can be changed, and this includes changing the electromagnetic pollution around us and in our homes. Once you raise your own level of consciousness, everything around you changes including detrimental energy, it rebalances itself. Trust and know this, otherwise fear will only attract that which you fear.

Once I have established the root cause, I can rebalance the energy. Although it is not essential for me to know the cause, my criteria is to rebalance whatever has gone on. As the work is remote, the client likes to know what the causes are.

Ways of healing a property

There are different ways of rebalancing your environment. Here are some of the choices:

+ **You can purchase a protective device for the home/ work.**

If you decide to do this check out how efficient these are. Many devices may help with balancing geopathic stress, but do not remove geopsychic stress on a person or within a home, so you may have to employ someone in this field

+ **You can employ someone to do this for you.**

Check their experience, track record, and professional qualifications, and make sure they are on a professional register such as the British Society of Dowsers, Canadian Society of Dowsers, American Society of Dowsers or other appropriate societies

Ensure someone can rebalance the energies of the whole property making it a safe place, and will help you do this for yourself. I don't believe keeping the way we work secret. Knowledge should be passed on

+ **Rebalance the energies yourself.**

Because the energies can be quite powerful, I recommend if you decide to do this, to undertake a professional training course that will not only teach you how to rebalance a property, but also protect and balance your own energies. The British Society of Dowsers and others worldwide do this, as well as myself, either online, one to one or in groups.

After working with a client which can be "on site'" or remotely, I send a report with my findings. On site and remotely both work equally well, but some clients like to watch how it is done and experience dowsing.

In the report I like to show people how to do the work for themselves, and ultimately how to keep their own energy clear and protected. A simple method to use daily on a property is to say the following Statement of Intent with feeling:

Rebalancing the energy of a property (or another's, with their permission)

"With Intent, I ask the divine healing energies and spirit of the place to work with my higher self, to bless and balance any non beneficial energies within this property, including any electrical appliances radiating unbalanced energy at source, for all the occupants as to their needs, for all who visit, pets, plants and other relevant life, now and in the future, as is appropriate, with infinite love and gratitude. So Be It."

The wording of the above can be changed to resonate with you. When people start working with these energies using the statement above it helps them focus, but it must be said with absolute feeling and trust, knowing this has happened. Visitors to a property, if in a negative state, can unknowingly bring disharmony to your home, so always rebalance the energies afterwards. If you feel like opening the windows and allowing good energy to flow in, that is fine, it is the intent behind it that is important.

After a house healing, I visualise an orb of golden reflective light around the property, with the intent this is keeping out any unbalanced energy, and protecting the already balanced energy within the home. I suggest to my clients to do this regularly, so these procedures are like cleaning your teeth. Protective if done regularly!

I would recommend doing this as often as you can. Your home is filled with energy and is energy. You can even talk to your house, and if you are going away, ask it to keep safe and protected! Don't think you are going mad by talking to your home! It is understanding we are all connected, so showing gratitude to your home for protecting you and your family is important. You have nothing to lose, so try it and see the difference.

Some of these techniques can be quite daunting to a newcomer, but once grasped can make a huge impact on their lives, creating a more balanced harmonious living environment.

Ultimately once we adopt the conscious living approach and raise the level of our awareness by being present, we change everything around us, but until then we need to work on ourselves and our environment.

Chapter 14

Surrender and Just Be!

This book is written to allow your consciousness to shift into a higher vibration, by looking at yourself and creating the life you want. In the past it took people years, even lifetimes, to transform their consciousness. We now live in a new consciousness with the opportunity to awaken now, just by *being*. My aim is to allow this to happen and not to fill the mind with new information and belief systems. The *awakening* will occur and guide those who are ready. Some are not ready, but people who are awakened will affect other people's consciousness.

Always remember we are human beings so allowed to have emotions, become stuck and confused. Try not to self-sabotage. The key is being aware, accepting, then moving on, doing the best you can at all times. If you fall off the path occasionally, don't self judge, accept it happened and keep on going.

Planet of Emotions

By the time this book is published we will be in the year 2012. We are in an earth school and on the planet of emotions. We have chosen to be here at this time in the earth's evolution as well as our own.

The planet goes through a new cycle every 26,000 years, and we are going into another 26,000 cycle now, so shifting into a higher consciousness. There is much talked about 2012, with many doom and gloom mongers out there. In the Mayan calendar 21st December 2012 is the end of the world, but this is not Armageddon.

It is the end of the world as we know it, but we are moving into a new era, new beginnings, with a new consciousness. The world has been filled with much fear, greed, and ego. It is this which has been destroying the planet, not global warming! It is time for us all to change now. We need to wake up to what we are really about, and I don't mean a load of new age rituals or "psychobabble."

This is real.

The place to start is within ourselves. We are all different in the way we learn and deal with life and this is why I have given options on how to deal with belief systems and emotions. There are no right or wrong ways in life, just different paths. Some people take longer than others, but my aim is to help you take a more direct route to awakening and find your true self. There are many spiritual paths, books, courses, and people telling you what to do. All the answers are within you, if you can find the stillness within. Listen, trust your inner voice and don't doubt.

Don't blame God when something goes wrong in your life or in the world. You are God, that infinite intelligence. We have created the mess we are in on the planet with pollution, a debt ridden economy and disease, but we have the ability to heal it.

We need to go back to living a more simplified life, without debt. This doesn't mean being without, or not having the luxuries in life. Eventually we will go back to a community way of living, helping others, caring and having respect for nature, living in peace and harmony within, with each other and the planet. All the great sages preached a spirituality of empathy, compassion, insisting people abandon egotism, greed, violence and unkindness.

In our society we have lost our admiration for the older generation. In many cultures they are respected and revered for their knowledge and wisdom. As a "young in mind" grandmother, I can assure you we will be returning to an age of respect for our elders and learn from them. Eckhart Tolle says old age is:

"A time of flowering of human consciousness"

It is time to develop a global consciousness, because whether we believe it or not, we live in one world. Practising compassion, empathy and forgiveness will ultimately lead to the evolution of our soul and the world.

Creating heaven on earth

There is still much talk and fear in some religions that if we do not mend our wicked ways we will go to hell, whilst the good among us will go to heaven. STOP NOW! Heaven is not a location high up in the sky where God resides. We can create our heaven on earth now. Eckhart Tolle, author of "A New Earth" says:

"We need to understand here that heaven is not a location but refers to the inner realm of consciousness. This is the esoteric meaning of the word, and this is also its meaning in the teachings of Jesus. Earth, on the other hand, is the outer manifestation in form, which is always a reflection of the inner. Collective human consciousness and life on our planet are intrinsically connected. 'A New Heaven' is the emergence of a transformed state of human consciousness, and 'A New Earth', is its reflection in the physical realm. Since human life and human consciousness are intrinsically one with the life of the planet, as the old consciousness dissolves, there are bound to be synchronistic geographic and climatic upheavals in many parts of the planet, some of which we are already witnessing."

So start now, creating within our lives, inner peace, harmony and love and this will become our experience of heaven on earth. We will carry this state of higher consciousness with us when our physical body dies. The true essence of who you are is not the physical body. This is just a vehicle to surround the soul, enabling us to evolve.

True happiness

This has been discussed before, so acts as a reminder. Happiness with most people is external and a role play. Behind someone's smiling façade may be sadness or depression. How many times have you heard people say, "I can't wait until my holidays, then I will be happy," or "When I move into a bigger house I will be happy," or "If I buy that sports car, I'll be really happy," only to find the novelty quickly wears off.

If you are unhappy it is a state of being, it is not who you are. If this happens and you feel depressed, say to yourself, "I accept the feeling of depression within me" and start watching your thoughts or write them down. What's behind them? Try the Emotional Transformation Process, and do the 11/22s as described in Chapter 3. You can accept the feeling and try to change, or just be miserable. Which will it be?

Positive and negative emotions

A negative emotion disrupts the flow of the body's balance and harmony. Fear, anger, jealousy, envy and guilt all disrupt the energy flow, affecting the immune system, heart and digestion. Mainstream medicine is now beginning to see the connection between the emotions and physical diseases.

Positive emotions, on the other hand, if not ego based, and have genuine deep feelings of inner peace and connectedness to source, will bring joy and love to your being.

Ego generated emotions which rely on external happiness can cause highs and lows. A wild night out partying, with lots of alcohol, may be fun at the time, but the following morning will bring a hangover and feelings of regret and unhappiness. This is an unstable way of living. It is all about balance. If you have a high, most definitely there will be a low. The ego likes to devalue the NOW, it thrives on us living in the past or worrying about the future.

Addictions

An addiction is usually an established, compulsive behavioural pattern that is difficult to control. Initially do not punish yourself and try to accept the situation. When you notice the compulsive need to have a cigarette, drink, reach for an extra piece of chocolate or go on a shopping spree, *stop*. Take in three deep breaths, which will bring you into total awareness. What is the feeling or emotion behind this? Take a few more breaths and see if the urge is still as great. With this practice of awareness, and following the Emotional Transformation Process, eventually this urge which is an energy field, the pain body, within you, will dissipate, but be patient and be aware of the body and how you are feeling.

Letting go of the past

Possibly one of the main causes of illness is the inability to let go of past events which bring back feelings of hurt, anger, guilt, frustration and loss. The human mind with its conditioning allows these emotions to block the flow of energy within the body, and if suppressed, eventually manifests as disease.

Our lifescript contains old emotions that are continually being revived. Our past is our memories, which are good and important to learn from. It is the thoughts from the past that keep playing like a gramophone record over and over again, until gradually the pain of this resentment, guilt or fear takes over. This emotional thinking has become who you are.

The secret is to break this pattern of dwelling on the past, by accepting it. Imagine yourself taking a step back out of the body and look at this emotion or feeling when it comes up, without judgment. Just stay detached and observe the energy of the feeling. How does it feel? This is not you. It is stuck old energy you have carried around like a sack of potatoes on your back, weighing you down and keeping you stuck in the past.

It is time to let go and dump this weight, so observe the energy and it will gradually dissipate until you feel yourself standing tall again, as if a weight has been lifted off your shoulders. If you struggle with this, talk to the feeling, just say, "I accept this feeling, it is not me, this is past stuck energy." Breathe deeply and let go and turn your attention to the present moment. Then you may experience a stillness, a deep inner peace.

It is possible you have experienced space between your thoughts. Once you are aware of these spaces and the immense peace that comes with them, a shift takes place, which is sometimes known as the "peace of God." The more you live in the present moment, the more you will experience and know the divine essence within you and who you really are.

When we do focus on our breathing, and notice the space between the in breath and out breath, it takes us away from thinking. Most people I come across shallow breathe, but can become aware of how deepening the breath brings them into the present moment, stops the thinking mind and brings stillness. When we are still we rise above our human reality and connect to our eternal being.

Start enjoying the simple things in life, be aware of the clouds that form in the sky, trees that blow in the wind, the birds swaying on the branches, or the rainfall upon the ground, (plenty in the UK!) Start paying attention to what's around you, as this will create a space, a gap. Initially you may not be aware of this, but it will come and create a feeling of inner peace.

This is *just being*, a feeling of complete oneness, a shift in consciousness, to become fully connected to everything around you and the universal intelligence which flows through your being.

When we stop asking ourselves, "Why is this happening to me?" we begin to accept and surrender.

My understanding of the past, present and future is it all exists simultaneously, just in different dimensions, and in 1952 Einstein wrote in his book, "Relativity":

"Since there exists in this four dimensional structure (space-time) no longer any sections which represent "now" objectively, the concepts of happening and becoming are indeed not completely suspended, but yet complicated.

It appears therefore more natural to think of physical reality as a four dimensional existence, instead of, as hitherto, the evolution of a three dimensional existence."

More on this will be in my next book, but until then, I have tried to think of a simple way of explaining this. The other day I had an AHA! moment when as a car passenger I was looking out of the window. I was admiring the beautiful blue sky full of fluffy white clouds. The clouds I was looking at through the window to my left were in that moment in the present. If I turned behind, looking over my left shoulder, the clouds were then in the past. If I looked ahead, the clouds were in the future, but all existed at the same time.

The main purpose of this book is to allow you to recognise the ego within you, and become aware of the habitual thoughts that envelop your life.

The Shift

Humanity and the earth are moving into a higher vibration or dimension. Dimensions are states of consciousness which we are all capable of moving into. Even if you are not aware of different dimensions you can still feel this *shift* that is happening around us.

The third dimension which most of us live in, is not who we are, and this way of living is constricting. It is about rigid rules, belief systems and limitations. Our lives revolve around the illusion of linear times-past, present and future-a 3D reality. Living in a 3D consciousness is very conditional. Some people have awakened and understand unconditional love and harmony. If this is the case you have moved up the ladder into a higher state of consciousness or dimension.

Much of humanity is still caught up in thoughts and unconscious limiting beliefs, which originate from our rational mind-the left brain, which uses only about 5% of the brains capacity. With the other 95% we have the ability to move into these higher states of consciousness right now, where there is only present time-the key to true happiness. In this state of being we observe everything around us in a detached way, and do not become attached to the thinking mind churning over and over past events and emotions.

In these higher states we reach a place where "Ask and you will Receive," happens instantaneously. You become the creator of your reality and manifest what you focus on. The ego has dissolved.

Initially when we start living more consciously and become aware, old suppressed thoughts and feelings arise. Don't panic, accept that this is your chance once and for all to release and let them go, do not suppress them just observe!

Daily watch the vibration of your thoughts and make sure they are not dark and gloomy, filled with negative television, fear, anger or hatred. Conversely ensure they are peaceful thoughts, such as flowers, trees or nature, a new born baby or whatever makes your heart sing-this has a lighter higher energy.

The more baggage we let go of the higher we fly! You have two choices-live a life being controlled by the 5% of the left brain, living in fear and the past, or be "YOU" using the brains full capacity-choose your thoughts and emotions in each moment, allowing them to flow by, moment by moment letting go-set yourself free and regain your power!

As your consciousness shifts you may find you attract new friends, others may drift away as your energy changes, or existing relationships may deepen. There may be a feeling of loneliness as if you're on your own, but this is only an illusion, a state of mind. It is because we have lost the connection to our true inner being, or connection to source.

You can either try participating in more external activities, or take yourself into nature and experience the oneness we have talked about and the reconnection to life. Talk to your loved ones that have passed over, as if they are sitting next to you, it's just you can't see them with the physical eyes, but trust me they are there only a thought away. Remember, where your thoughts and attention go, your energy follows, so you are communicating on an energetic level. Ask questions, the answers will come, sometimes in the form of a distant memory. The communication has started!

Deeper awareness of life opens the doorway to a sense we and all life are connected. You start to realise underneath a person's physical façade is a beautiful soul. Next time you look into someone's eyes see the beauty of their soul, their being. As I have said before, we may not like, the personality of a person or feel uneasy in their presence. We don't have to be their best friend, but they are no better or worse than anyone else.

With this new rise in consciousness and empowerment, we are not putting up with abuse, inequality and greed, whereas in the past it may have been swept under the carpet. We can see this happening around the world at present. There can be no secrets anymore.

Your inner self or soul is the infinite you, so connect daily, through meditation or awareness and *just being*, then you can tune into the abundance of love, peace, harmony and intelligence.

Once the busy over-stimulated mind is quietened, we have the realisation that we are connected to each other and the cosmos, like a giant invisible web. We need to work in harmony to benefit the whole. Animals realise this connection more than us and rarely do they die in natural disasters. Usually they disappear several days before, because they listen to their intuitive warning of danger. This happened in the Tsunami in 2004.

Conclusion

Many of us self-judge or self-sabotage, causing a great deal of pain to ourselves. You can change. You may catch yourself every now and again telling the same old story. The difference now is hopefully you will start to be aware. Be loving and compassionate to yourself. Follow these rules and remind yourself daily:

- You are not a victim
- De-clutter your life
- Speak your truth
- Breathe deeply
- Exercise regularly
- Eat a balanced alkali diet
- Live in the present
- Listen
- Be aware
- Listen to your heart and not the head
- Be mindful
- Be discerning
- Live from your heart not the mind
- Watch your thoughts
- Have forgiveness
- Acceptance of everything in life
- Have fun and laughter
- Stop criticism
- Blame no-one else for your situation
- Be non judgemental
- Live with no ego
- Observe and stay detached

- Protect and clear your energy

- As humans we have free will, ask and you will receive!

- Surrender and just be

If you can surrender to all that is, accept the present moment and *just be*, you attain true happiness and nothing external can change your internal feelings. True happiness is not something that comes to you externally through possessions, a relationship, career, or waiting for a lottery win. It is the consciousness within that harnesses true happiness, and who you really are. The list above is the best way you can live your life, ultimately, staying present and mindful.

Once we become aware of our inner body, knowing daily how it feels, we become aware that a greater intelligence is present. When we realise we didn't create our body this intelligence did, the same intelligence that created nature, we become more alive.

Life is about co-operation and not competition. Connecting, not competing.

You have the key to true happiness, joy, freedom and truth, so unlock the door, enter, and then spread your light to others!

Surrender to life and allow intelligence to flow through you. Let go and allow the shift in human consciousness.

A new world is here. You have the power beyond your imagination to transform and co-create your life and this new earth.

THE TIME IS NOW!

References

Electromagnetic Field Solutions:
www.earthing.com
www.dulwichhealth.com
www.emfields.org
www.powerwatch.org

Health
www.drbriffa.com
www.cholesteroltruth.com
www.credence.org
www.detox4life.com.au
www.dulwichhealth.com
www.healerfound.co.uk
www.infinitebeing.com
www.ewg.org/skindeep.com
www.marilynglenville.com
www.thenha.co.uk
www.phmiracleliving.com
www.psionmedicine.org
www.mercola.com
www.normshealy.com
www.saveourbones.com
www.wddty.com
www.lynnemctaggart.com

General
www.infinitebeing.com
www.electrocrystal.com
www.ewg.org
www.inluminoglobal.co.uk

www.valeriehunt.com
www.brucelipton.com
www.eckharttolle.com
www.noetic.org
www.spiritrelease.com

Dowsing
British Society Of Dowsers:
www.britishdowsers.org
American Society Of Dowsers:
www.dowsers.org
Canadian Society Of Dowsers:
www.canadiandowsers.org

Recommended Reading

Dowsing
Elizabeth Brown, Dowsing, Hay House
Christopher Bird, The Diving Hand, E.P. Dutton
British Society of Dowsers, The Journal of the British Society of Dowsers
Susan Collins, Bridge Matter and Spirit with Dowsing
Tom Graves, The Diviners Handbook,
Joey Korn, Dowsing: A Path to Enlightenment
Patrick MacManaway MD Energy Dowsing for Everyone
Hamish Miller, The Definitive Wee Book on Dowsing, Penwith Press
Dale W. Olsen, The New Pendulum Charts

Geopathic Stress
Kathe Bachler, Earth Radiation, Wordmasters Ltd
Dr Edith Fiore, The Unquiet Dead, Ballantine Books
Rolf Gordon, Are You Sleeping in a Safe Place?
Jane Thurnell Reid, Geopathic Stress and Subtle Energies
Ober, Sinatra MD, Zucker, Earthing, The Most Important Health
    Discovery Yet.

Health
Barbara Brennan, Hands Of Light
Colin Campbell, The China Study
Dr Hulde Clark, The Cure Of All Diseases
Patrick Holford, The New Optimum Nutrition Bible
M .Verbach, Healing Through Nutrition

General
Brandon Bays, The Journey
William Bloom, Psychic Protection
Dr. Deepak Chopra, Quantum Healing, Seven Spiritual Laws Of Success
Dr Susan Cabot, The Liver Cleansing Diet

Colin Campbell, China Study, (comprehensive study of nutrition)
Dr Wayne Dyer, The Power Of Intention
Gregg Braden, The Divine Matrix
Bryan Hubbard, Time-Light
Dr Masaru Emoto, The Hidden Messages in Water
Udo Erasmus, Fats That Heal, Fats That Kill
Louise Hay, I Can Do It
Dr David Hamilton, How Your Mind Can Heal Your Body
Dr Valerie Hunt, Uncork Your Consciousness
Dr Susan Jeffers, Feel The Fear and Do It Anyway, End The Struggle and
    Dance With Life
Bruce H. Lipton, PhD. The Biology of Belief, Hay House
Lynne McTaggart, The Field, The Bond, Harper Collins
Claire Montanaro, Spiritual Wisdom
Mike Robinson, The True Dynamics of Life, True Dynamics of Relationships
John Ruskan, Emotional Clearing
Dr Bernie Siegel, Love, Medicine and Miracles
Professor Chris Sinha, Journal Of Language and Cognition
Neale Donald Walsh, Conversations With God
Owen Waters, The Shift
Eckhart Tolle, The Power of Now, A New Earth

SANDRA KENDREW offers online courses and talks on:
Transformation through Dowsing
Healing Yourself, Others and Your Environment
Emotional Transformation Process
Conscious Living
Others to be confirmed
www.thehousehealer.co.uk
www.sandrakendrew.co.uk
Email sandrakendrew@hotmail.co.uk to be on my mailing list for an update
    on information or products.

Lightning Source UK Ltd.
Milton Keynes UK
UKOW051124060312

188441UK00001B/55/P